New Bodleian – making the Weston Library

D0589448

With Best Wishes

Jim

Many thanks,

Geoff

New Bodleian – making the Weston Library

Bodleian Library
UNIVERSITY OF OXFORD

in association with WilkinsonEyre and Mace

The Bodleian Libraries are one of the glories of the world of learning. They lie at the very heart of the university both geographically and metaphorically, by providing material and digital collections, which are the most basic resources of any community of scholars and students.

As the main library of the university, the Bodleian is also an international library of the highest rank. From the very beginning, it has opened its doors not just to members of the university but to readers from far afield who came to consult its rich holdings. Over four centuries later, the Bodleian continues to draw readers from across the globe. Today, more than half its readership is from outside the university.

The founder, Sir Thomas Bodley, envisioned that his library, founded in 1602, would one day need new buildings to house its growing collection. His example of endowing the Old Schools Quadrangle (begun in 1610), vastly extending the original reading room built for Duke Humfrey's books in 1488, was followed by John Radcliffe, who endowed the Radcliffe Camera (completed 1749). To these were added the New Bodleian Library, funded by the Rockefeller Foundation, and the Radcliffe Science Library in the twentieth century.

Through continued generous benefaction, the renovated New Bodleian, now known as the Weston Library, has been transformed into an exceptional special collections library, capable of safely housing and preserving the Bodleian's great treasures and making its outstanding holdings available to scholars and visitors alike.

The story of the remarkable transformation of the building outlined in the pages of this book is a testament to the generosity, vision, technical skill and tireless commitment of the many individuals who have collectively given Oxford an outstanding new library fit for the twenty-first century. Together, they have helped to ensure that Bodley's Republic of Letters will continue to flourish for generations to come.

Professor Louise Richardson
Vice-Chancellor, University of Oxford

It has been my great pleasure to watch this building develop, from the simple drawing I first saw to this magnificent space. The new Weston Library is a remarkable building which embodies many of the causes with which my family and the Garfield Weston Foundation have been involved.

First and foremost, the Weston Library is a centre for research and education. Through the beautifully appointed reading and seminar rooms, readers now have an opportunity to consult the Bodleian's unique collections in what are undoubtedly the best possible conditions for doing so in the 400-year history of the library. Students can now come face to face with collections as part of their education in a controlled environment.

It has also given staff a place to look after the collections of the Bodleian, carefully preserving a significant part of our shared heritage for generations to come.

The creative renovation of the building has resulted in new spaces for the public, drawing in the community to engage with the Bodleian's collections through its new exhibition halls, lecture theatre and other public spaces.

Thomas Bodley's wish in 1602 for his newly opened library is immortalized in a plaque above the entrance to the Old Library which reads 'May it turn out well' (*Quod feliciter vortat*). My wish for the Weston Library is the same: may it serve as an inspiration for staff, students, readers and visitors for years to come.

Guy Weston
Chairman, Garfield Weston Foundation

Oxford University's determination to live up to its claim that it is 'the greatest university in the world for thinking' is nowhere more clearly evidenced than in the renovation of the New Bodleian to create the Weston Library. For Bodley's Librarian Richard Ovenden, it is 'what we have been put on the planet to do', while for architect Jim Eyre it is one of the projects he is most proud of. Together they have not only transformed a dour and forbidding building into a welcoming centre of scholarship where some of the greatest scholars in the world will gather to play intellectual tennis, but have also created rich opportunities for extending this discourse beyond the library's walls to involve the general public.

The project is a unique example of what can happen when a small team implement an inspired vision with dedication and a good measure of love, and it is no wonder that their backers and supporters are unanimous in agreeing that they have surpassed every expectation.

Toby Blackwell
President, Blackwell's Bookshops

Contents

The Weston Library

Commentary
Robert Bevan

Libraries are without parallel as repositories of cultural memory and, consequently, of cultural identity. This is why their creation can excite comment and debate like few other building types beyond the personalized domain of the house – the place of intense private memory. The destruction of libraries has, equally, alarmed both their contemporaneous host societies and successor societies down the centuries: Alexandria, Louvain, Sarajevo, the manuscript libraries of Timbuktu or Charles Rennie Mackintosh's Glasgow School of Art – generations of culture can turn to ash in hours. Fire is the devourer of rare books; ancient treatises on diplomacy, necromancy or philosophy; cadastral records that link people to place; lost alphabets and maps of new-found lands.

It's only recently that Giles Gilbert Scott's, in retrospect, unconscionably cavalier handling of Britain's cultural record has come to light. An inveterate straddler of fences, Scott's desire to meld the traditional with the functional saw the New Bodleian built, in the medieval fashion, as a Bladon rubble curtain wall surrounding an eleven-storey keep. The keep encased a forest of steel L-sections set in pairs that not only supported the building itself but, directly, 117 miles of shelving containing the country's history.

Unfortunately, this structurally efficient system was too clever by half, with the gaps between the paired steels and between floors effectively turning the entire eleven storeys of the stack into one compartment. The nation's largest and most important collection of books and papers after the British Library was effectively housed in a chimney.

Not only that but Scott then installed furnaces in the basement of the building to heat not only the New Bodleian itself but also the old Bodleian and various other university buildings. Assessments suggested that if a fire did break out there was a one in three chance of total structural collapse and the loss of the entire collection. WilkinsonEyre's re-imagining of one of Scott's least successful creations had to address both the building's vices and virtues, and couldn't have come too soon.

The New Bodleian can't help but disappoint on first acquaintance and not just for its potential incendiary qualities. Its medieval massing forms the armature for an essentially neo-classical building, albeit one with modernist strip windows and refracted through a vaguely art deco lens. Architectural historian Howard Colvin once described the building as 'a dinner jacket made of Harris Tweed'. But Scott was not to be persuaded away from the centrist line set out in his inaugural speech as RIBA president: 'I hold no brief either for the extreme diehard Traditionalist or the extreme Modernist and it seems idle to compare styles and say that one is better than another.'

Some critics have seen Scott, questionably, as on the same architectural arc that extends from the national romanticism of Ragnar Östberg (Stockholm City Hall) to the proto-critical regionalism of Willem Marinus Dudok or, in the UK, Reginald Uren's Hornsey Town Hall which had just won the Royal Institute of British Architects (RIBA) Bronze Medal when the New Bodleian plans were unveiled. But, compared to the contemporary works published in the same titles, such as Arne Jacobsen's indoor tennis club near Copenhagen or various Czech Functionalist housing estates, Scott's work is, undoubtedly, towards the rear-guard of architecture's modernist march.

However, that does not make Scott an unusually conservative designer for his period. Even a glance at the May 1936 issues of the architectural journals that published Scott's Bodleian proposals show him to have been in the mainstream. That year's architecture room at the Royal Academy's summer exhibition included images of public buildings such as Thomas Tait's government buildings in Edinburgh as well as Bury Town Hall and municipal offices in Hertfordshire, Watford and Wood Green that were, superficially, in much the same idiom as Scott's New Bodleian work – a kind of stretched classical municipal moderne.

When it came to this architectural peloton, Scott was no straggler, always keen to use the latest technologies and solutions – whether it be a highly efficient steel structure or pneumatics and conveyors to move requests and books speedily around the Bodleian complex. Where Scott really came into his own, though, was in the innovative massing of his buildings and the New Bodleian is no exception.

After the triumph of Scott's Cambridge University Library with its powerfully massed and modelled tower (that continues his work at Liverpool's Anglican cathedral and anticipates that at Bankside), the massing of the New Bodleian may appear quotidian, whereas it is ingenious.

Scott's much praised Cambridge library project had the distinct advantage of not being forced to negotiate a tight city centre site – likewise, Liverpool had its eminence above a hill and Bankside an industrial riverfront. In Oxford, Scott had to negotiate a built-up corner in the heart of a historic city, paying due regard to heights and relating the new building to the exquisite sequence of Bodleian buildings and other distinguished neighbours such as Wren's Sheldonian Theatre. All this while anticipating the provision of enough shelving for two further centuries of acquisitions.

In the latter, Scott may have been over-ambitious, but he succeeded brilliantly in fitting an eleven-storey building into a city that had already firmly ruled out skyscrapers – indeed it had imposed a maximum height limit of 50 feet on all new buildings so as not to overtop Carfax Tower, the tallest building in central

Oxford at 74 feet. The New Bodleian's stack is 78 feet high, exceeding the city limit by more than 50 per cent, but it is so cleverly screened by wings of reading rooms and offices that it barely intrudes on the skyline even in long views along Broad Street where its balustrade appears as no more than the parapet of one of the larger university departments.

In his essay (see page 80), Jim Eyre writes about the care that Scott took to set back the bulk of the New Bodleian from Broad Street to open up the space in front of the Clarendon Building and Sheldonian. One could also argue that with his south staircase tower and the recessed curve at the corner of Broad Street and Parks Road, Scott is responding to the sequence of curves in the townscape and their interplay with nearby orthogonal buildings projecting into space positively and negatively – the external corners of projecting wings and the internal corners of quads. This not only involves large-scale landmarks such as the Radcliffe Camera and the Sheldonian, but small-scale details such as the curve and cupola of Basil Champneys' old Indian Institute diagonally opposite the New Bodleian.

Less successful is the choice of the rubble-faced Bladon stone and how this is handled at ground level in particular. Perhaps Scott was wishing to emphasize the building's primarily utilitarian purpose with his rustic choice? Or perhaps this was his Oxford version of the moderne habit of using massy brick in the modern manner in conjunction with deco or classical details in stone. Hornsey Town Hall is one example of this modern approach and, more pertinently, Liverpool Philharmonic Hall by Herbert Rowse with its vertical blades and curved staircase towers is another.

Rowse's concert hall was commissioned at much the same time as the New Bodleian and there is much overlap between the Rowse and Scott aesthetics. Scott was one of the assessors of the 1923 competition for Liverpool's India Buildings that Rowse

Previous page:
The new Weston Library from
Catte Street.

Scott's south facade, remodelled and
open to the public.

won and the latter's 1930s designs for the Mersey Tunnel ventilation buildings owe much to Scott's earlier work at Battersea. Certainly, A.S.G. Butler's idea of the New Bodleian as 'neo-Jacobean' seems wide of the mark.

Scott himself described the New Bodleian thus: 'I favour a modern building that does pay some respect to the traditions that produced the old buildings round about. Stone-faced walls seemed essential for this purpose. The general massing and fenestration, however, might well be modern in character, the result being an entirely plain block, with a modern pattern of window openings ... Ornament has, in fact, only been used where it serves a definite aesthetic purpose, and not applied indiscriminately merely to enrich the building.'

Scott's decision to wrap the street frontages of the New Bodleian in a forbidding semi-blind arcade with high-level window cills may have been appropriate to its utilitarian function – in this case storage rather than power generation or ventilation – but it created a dead frontage on an otherwise lively street. It is a screening device similar to that which Scott used for his defensive facade at Bristol Corporation Electricity Department (1933). But many of the building's projections and set backs bore no relation to the internal arrangements. One early critic compared these external ridges to those found on the spine of an old-fashioned book to hold the binding chords in place – 'an outmoded piece of artiness' was the judgement.

It's appropriate then that the visitor's initial experience of WilkinsonEyre's bold intervention begins on the library's south side where the relationship of the library to its context has been transformed. The main move here has been to open up the blank facade to create an entrance arcade using the existing bays whose stone pilasters have then been carefully remodelled as pillars. A glazed screen with entrance doors (suitably set back within the arcade to avoid glassy intrusion into a set-piece street scene) reverses the building's hostility to outsiders and becomes something of a university first in welcoming the general public into its more usually exclusive confines.

The remodelling of this facade also allows for the removal of the ungainly plinth that projected from the south side of the New Bodleian and replaces it with steps that are shallow enough to avoid the need for handrails. Scott's purpose in providing this curving plinth along the back of the pavement is unclear but appears to be the vestige of an earlier iteration of the proposals that included a staff canteen in the building's southerly projecting wing that would have had doors onto a patio area in front of the building. This doesn't sound like a satisfactory arrangement either, whereas a high garden wall with planting behind would at least have had the air of an off-limits college garden in the Oxford manner. In any case, the plinth's removal is a small but surprisingly important gain for the building.

WilkinsonEyre's new entrance screen leads into the soaring Blackwell Hall, a central orientation space that, with the removal of the bulk of the books off site, has created a void in place of Scott's solid stacks and, in doing so, creates an internal quad with a shop and exhibition and auditorium spaces leading off it to the north. These moves have turned the building inside out – creating something partially porous from a structure that was previously largely hermetic.

For the public, the business of the special collections library goes on above you, glimpsed through a variety of glazed openings including a pair of elevated glazed corridor-bridges that form a twenty-first century cloister.

Something of Scott's original storage concept is acknowledged in the form of WilkinsonEyre's 'floating stack' that hovers within the

revealed void, surrounded by slots down which light pours. It contains shelving for accessible items and the visiting scholars' centre. The move is informed by the King's Library at the British Museum and the Beinecke Library at Yale – but with the dramatics of gilded book spines or the latter's flaming alabaster eschewed. The Weston Library is a working building not a ceremonial centre and so the floating stack is no 'holy of holies' for the veneration of literary relics as at Gordon Bunshaft's Beinecke (or Richard MacCormac's Ruskin Library at Lancaster). Too dramatic a gesture could have usurped the rightful heart of the Bodleian complex that remains at Duke Humfrey's Library.

Instead, the stack's discreetly canted walls interact quietly with the light penetrating down through Scott's characteristic slots and the warm glow given off by the retained clerestory windows (like those at Battersea) that now sit high on the southern face of the hall's perimeter.

Of course, Scott's building wasn't entirely devoted to storage, but the role of its reading rooms, once rather peripheral to the main Bodleian event, have become central to the Weston as the home of the Bodleian's special collections – no more precious books jiggling apart along the underground conveyor belt to the Old Bodleian or being tucked under the arm for a dash across a rainy street.

WilkinsonEyre's restoration of the existing reading rooms and its provision of additional spaces for readers will transform perceptions of the building from its role as a support act to a fully integrated element of the Bodleian. In the process, Scott was unnecessarily defensive about his *gesamtkunstwerk* approach, saying: 'Ornament, in fact, has only been used where it serves a definite aesthetic purpose, and not applied indiscriminately merely to enrich the building.' This was never true but the restoration has revealed its richness once more – from bronzed

screens formerly hidden behind partitions to finial-like doorknobs and wood chandeliers. It is ornament that now offers a subtle grandeur to the building's enhanced status.

WilkinsonEyre has also continued in Scott's experimental tradition where appropriate, such as with the insertion of the double-height centre for visiting scholars where a communal space for cross-disciplinary exchange sits alongside stacked rooms as private carrels.

Creating the new Charles Wendell David Penthouse Reading Room has not only restored Scott's carefully calculated external volumes and, with the removal of the Indian Institute extension, banished an intrusion from Oxford's skyline, it has also provided a roof terrace with one of the UK's most magical panoramas across the rooftops of the city.

What WilkinsonEyre has not been as keen to reinstate is the New Bodleian's tortuous circulation pattern. This is easier said than done. Scott's parti was basically a square within a square, a filled-in quad with no readily accessible routes through the middle. It was never an easy building to navigate and this architectural failing was clear from the start with, in May 1936, *The Architect and Building News* commenting on Scott's proposals: 'The most obvious criticism is of the layout of the readers' entrances, passageways and stairways.' The journal noted that the staircase up to the PPE (now the Rare Books and Manuscripts) Reading Room 'is 130ft from the Broad Street entrance and obscurely placed in relation to the Parks Road entrance ... this in-articulated communication is a serious fault'.

This is not simply an issue expressed internally. Scott clearly felt the need to create a ceremonial entrance on the Broad Street elevation to terminate the (slightly skewed) axis through the Old Bodleian along what has come to be called the 'Pevsner Walk'.

With the redundant Broad Street plinth removed, the entrance steps are now a place for visitors to linger.

View inside the Weston's new entrance arcade, showing the glazed screen set back behind the remodelled original pilasters.

This entrance was rarely if ever used for the purpose, and its vaulted stone vestibule became a cupboard at the end of the long east corridor with readers using the Parks Road entrance instead.

WilkinsonEyre's new arcade and elevated glass corridors together with new lifts and staircase cores go some way to improving the circulation situation, but entirely unpicking the original problem that Scott set up has not proved easy. Indeed, it is a problem made harder still to resolve by the introduction of the interested public into parts of the building, in addition to the readers and library staff. In this conflicting desire to open up the building and yet keep its contents safe there are still some instances where architectural methods cannot be used to resolve the situation Scott originally set up – visitors to the building's staff offices, for example, will need to be escorted. Security is a significant and growing concern in such a treasure house and there were some high-profile thefts of rare books from the library in the decade before it closed for remodelling. Such matters have had to be considered even in the furniture, with Scott's reading room tables adapted so that any papers in use can be more readily supervised.

We live in a very different world from Scott's but Giles Gilbert could be surprisingly visionary. In the future, he once speculated, 'libraries as we know them will have ceased to exist, and a central television station will wireless visions of books to readers' homes and they will turn the pages by pressing a button!' Not that far off the mark, even if we now know that each fresh communications technology tends to complement, rather than replace, existing media. To talk of Scott as cavalier in his approach to the fire risk in the library is, on reflection, unfair; he thought he was doing the right thing. He built a library storage facility that used the most modern methods then available (including aluminium windows that are still doing their job just fine and hollow pot partition walls

to some rooms to ease their later change of use). He was an innovator as well as a traditionalist.

Given the extremely tough archival standards demanded today with fire compartments within fire compartments deemed necessary and levels of servicing and security unimaginable to Scott, to demolish the building entirely and start again wouldn't have been an entirely unreasonable suggestion. But as WilkinsonEyre and others have found, the New Bodleian demands a slow-appreciation of its discreet charms. It also has importance because of its place in Giles Gilbert Scott's oeuvre, even if his ideas were more successfully executed elsewhere. Gavin Stamp has described it (and Scott's Cambridge University Library) as: 'the [work] of a resourceful designer trying to respond with intelligence and integrity to changing conditions and new technologies while respecting the character of both ancient university towns'. This seems fair.

WilkinsonEyre has now saved and improved upon the best of Scott's work at the New Bodleian, most notably the volumetric skills he displayed at all scales, whether phone box or cathedral, as well as the character of its generous and decorative reading rooms. More fundamentally the new New Bodleian has provided something both useful and beautiful – a safe casket for the nation's literary treasures.

The Blackwell Hall is now a democratic, public space, an internal quadrangle which pedestrians are free to enter from Broad Street.

To the north side of the Blackwell Hall, the void is narrow, and spanned by glazed footbridges into the stack.

A glazed ribbon of books wrap around the Blackwell Hall below the floating, timber-clad stack volume.

Looking up from the Blackwell Hall, the slender roof-lights and slots into the central stack echo Scott's trademark vertical strip windows.

Openings into the perimeter walls of the Blackwell Hall provide glimpses of the working library within. Some are simple window units; others have an intimate seat in the manner of a monastery cloister.

In the east wing, Scott's original corridor – now refurbished – gives access to new meeting and seminar rooms, and the restored reading rooms at first floor level.

At first floor level, existing rooms have been replaced by a new, more informal, breakout space and enquiries area for readers, flanked by meeting and seminar rooms.

The double-height central space of the Visiting Scholars' Centre now hosts informal meetings and other gatherings which encourage collaboration among library staff and visiting academics.

Following pages:
The original bronze screen of the Mackerras Reading Room frames views into the refurbished space beyond.

In the Rare Books and Manuscripts Reading Room, most of the original features were designed by Scott specifically for the space. These have been restored and, in some cases, refurbished to suit the changing demands of readers and the increased use of technology.

Slender vertical windows alternate with timber shelf units in the south wall of the David Reading Room – the top floor of Scott's 'castle keep'.

Beyond the vertical windows of the David Reading Room, the external terrace gives a unique vantage point for sweeping views across Oxford's 'dreaming spires'.

The context

A brief history of the Bodleian
Geoffrey Tyack

The first library for Oxford University – as distinct from the colleges – was housed in a room above the Old Congregation House, begun c.1320 on a site to the north of the chancel of the University Church of St Mary the Virgin. The building stood at the heart of Oxford's 'academic quarter', close to the schools in which lectures were given. The library was built with funds supplied by Thomas de Cobham, Bishop of Worcester, but was still unfinished when he died in 1327. The room, which still exists as a vestry and meeting room for the church, is neither large nor architecturally impressive, and it was superseded in 1488 by the library known as Duke Humfrey's, which constitutes the oldest part of the Bodleian complex. The occasion for moving to a new building was the gift to the university by Humfrey, Duke of Gloucester, younger brother of King Henry V, of his priceless collection of more than 281 manuscripts, including several important classical texts. These volumes would have made the existing library desperately overcrowded, and in 1444 the university decided to erect a new library over the Divinity School, begun in about 1424 on a site at the northern end of School Street, just inside the town wall. Because of chronic shortages of funds the building was still unfinished in the 1440s, and the library was not begun in earnest until 1478; it was finally opened ten years later.

Duke Humfrey's Library survived in its original form for just over sixty years; in 1550 it was denuded of its books after a visitation by Richard Cox, Dean of the newly founded Christ Church. He was acting under legislation passed by King Edward VI designed to purge the English church of all traces of Roman Catholicism, including 'superstitious books and images'. In the words of the historian Anthony Wood, 'some of those books so taken out by the Reformers were burnt, some sold away for Robin Hood's pennyworths, either to Booksellers, or to Glovers to press their gloves, or Taylors to make measures, or to Bookbinders to cover books bound by them, and some also kept by the Reformers for their own use'. Oxford University was not a wealthy institution and did not have the resources to build up a collection of new printed books to replace those dispersed. Therefore, in 1556 the desks were sold, and the room was taken over by the Faculty of Medicine.

The library was rescued by Sir Thomas Bodley (1545–1613), a fellow of Merton College who had travelled extensively in Europe and had, between 1585 and 1596, carried out several diplomatic missions for Queen Elizabeth I. He married a rich widow whose husband had made a fortune from trading in pilchards and, in his retirement from public life, decided, in his own words, to 'set up my staff at the library door in Oxon; being thoroughly persuaded, that in my solitude, and surcease from the Commonwealth affairs, I could not busy myself to better purpose, than by reducing that place (which then in every part lay ruined and waste) to the public use of students'. His money was accepted in 1598, and the old library was refurbished to house a new collection of some 2,500 books, some of them given by Bodley himself, some by other donors. A librarian, Thomas James, was appointed, and the library finally opened on 8 November 1602. The first printed catalogue followed in 1605; a new edition of 1620 ran to 675 pages.

In 1610, Bodley entered into an agreement with the Stationers' Company of London under which a copy of every book published in England and registered at Stationers' Hall would be deposited in the new library. Although at first the agreement was honoured more in the breach than in the observance, it nevertheless pointed to the future of the library as a comprehensive and ever-expanding collection, different in both size and purpose from

Site of the Bodleian Library and Radcliffe Square from the north, from Ralph Agas's 1578 map of Oxford. The site of the Weston Library is in the bottom right-hand corner of the map.

The Divinity School and Duke Humfrey's Library, as drawn by John Bereblock in 1566.

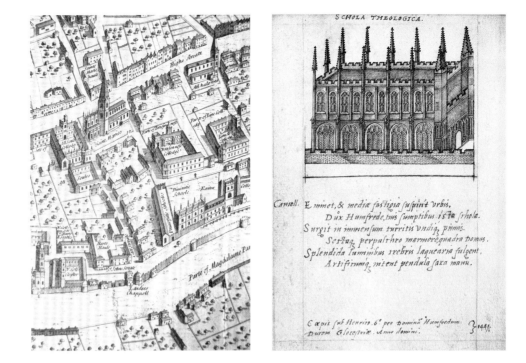

David Loggan's 1675 drawing of the Arts and Selden End extensions to Duke Humfrey's Library.

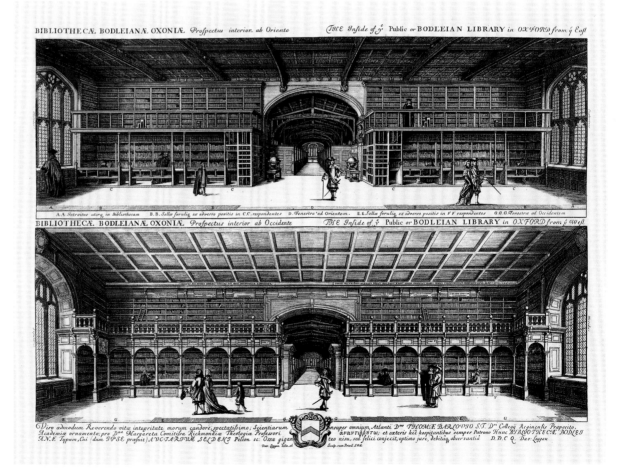

the libraries of the colleges. More immediately it imposed an extra strain on space within the building, which was already housing many more books than originally foreseen; new gifts of books made the lack of space ever more acute. So in 1610–12 Bodley planned and financed the first extension to the medieval building, known as Arts End.

Bodley died in 1613 and, on the day after his funeral, work started on the building of a spacious quadrangle of buildings (the Schools Quadrangle) to the east of the library. Bodley was the prime mover in this ambitious project, but most of the money was raised by loans and public subscription. The buildings were designed to house lecture and examination rooms ('schools' in Oxford parlance) to replace what Bodley called 'those ruinous little rooms' on the site in which generations of undergraduates had been taught. In his will Bodley left money to add a third floor designed to serve as 'a very large supplement for stowage of books', which also became a public museum and picture gallery, the first in England. The quadrangle was structurally complete by 1619, but work on fitting it out continued until at least 1624.

The last addition to Bodley's buildings came in 1634–7, when another extension to Duke Humfrey's Library was built; still known as Selden End, after the lawyer John Selden (1584–1654) who made a gift of 8,000 books which were housed there, it stands at the far end of the Divinity School, over the Convocation House, the meeting-room for the university's 'Parliament'. The library was now able to receive and house numerous gifts of books and, especially, manuscripts: from the 3rd Earl of Pembroke in 1629; from Sir Kenelm Digby in 1634; from William Laud, Archbishop of Canterbury, starting in 1635; and from many others.

It was the collections of manuscripts, as much as those of books, which attracted scholars from all over Europe, irrespective of whether or not they were members of the University of Oxford, a tradition which the Bodleian still keeps up (undergraduates, on the other hand, were rarely admitted until quite recent times). Another tradition, still zealously guarded, is that no books were to be lent to readers; even King Charles I was refused permission to borrow a book in 1645. But the number of users should not be overestimated; in 1831 there was an average of three or four readers a day, and there were no readers at all in July. With no heating until 1845 and no artificial lighting until 1929, the library only opened from 10 a.m. to 3 p.m. in the winter and 9 a.m. to 4 p.m. in the summer.

The growth of the collection slowed down in the early eighteenth century when the library, like the university as a whole, entered into a somewhat somnolent period; no books at all were purchased between 1700 and 1703. Yet the late seventeenth and early eighteenth centuries saw a spate of library-building in Oxford. Most of the new libraries were built by the colleges, but the finest of all, at least from an architectural point of view, was the brainchild of an individual, Dr John Radcliffe (1650–1714), perhaps the most successful English physician of his day. He left his trustees a large sum of money with which to purchase both the land for the new building and an endowment to pay a librarian and to purchase books. The site eventually chosen was to the south of the Schools Quadrangle, in the middle of a new square (Radcliffe Square) formed by the demolition of old houses in School Street and Catte Street and bounded by All Souls and Brasenose Colleges and the University Church. Here, between 1737 and 1748, the monumental circular domed building –

Interior view of Duke Humfrey's Library with the stall-system shelving, installed during the 1598 refurbishment.

Oxford's most impressive piece of classical architecture – went up to the designs of James Gibbs, and it was finally opened in 1749.

For many years the Radcliffe Library, as it was called until 1860, was something of a white elephant. It was completely independent of the Bodleian, readers were few in number, the heterogeneous collection of books served no obvious purpose, and the first librarians displayed a strange reluctance to add to it. Matters improved in the early nineteenth century, when a collection of books on medicine and natural history was gradually amassed: something celebrated by the publication of the first printed catalogue in 1835. Meanwhile the Bodleian's collections had begun to grow again. Successive pieces of legislation made the agreement with the Stationers' Company more effective, so that by 1842 the library could concentrate its purchases on manuscripts and foreign books, secure in the knowledge that new books published in England would be deposited free of charge. Gifts of books and manuscripts continued to be made, notably that of 18,000 printed books (including 300 incunabula – books printed before 1500) and 393 manuscripts from the bequest of Francis Douce in 1834. In 1849, six years after the publication of a new catalogue in three folio volumes, there were estimated to be 220,000 books and some 21,000 manuscripts in the library's collection.

The Bodleian was not only a collection of books and manuscripts; it also housed pictures, sculptures, coins and medals, and 'curiosities': objects of scientific, exotic or historical interest, including a stuffed crocodile from Jamaica. Old pictures show these eclectic collections in different parts of the present library buildings, but especially in the gallery on the top floor of the Schools Quadrangle. In 1755 the collections were augmented by the Countess of Pomfret's gift of a large part of the Arundel Marbles, the first collection of antique statuary to be formed in England. They were housed in two of the ground-floor rooms around the quadrangle no longer needed for teaching. Starting in 1788, the rooms on the first floor were given over to library use, including the storage of manuscripts, and with the opening of the University Galleries – now the Ashmolean Museum – in Beaumont Street in 1845 the marbles were transferred to a more suitable setting, as were seventy pictures from the top-floor gallery. This left more space for storing books, which was further increased in 1859 when the university agreed to relinquish the last of its ground-floor lecture rooms; they were rehoused in 1876–82 in the new Examination Schools in the High Street. With its completion, the whole of the Schools Quadrangle was at last in the hands of the library, save for two rooms in the tower in which the Oxford University archives were kept.

A further increase in space came about in 1860, when the Radcliffe Library was taken over by the Bodleian and renamed the Radcliffe Camera (the word *camera* means 'room' in Latin). The upper-floor library became a reading room, used mainly by undergraduates, who had been admitted to the Bodleian since 1856, and the ground floor was turned into a bookstack (it was

converted into a second reading room in 1941). Thus the library acquired its first major addition of space for readers since the building of Selden End in 1634; by the beginning of the twentieth century an average of a hundred people a day were using it. The medical and scientific books formerly kept in the Radcliffe Camera were moved to new premises in the University Museum in South Parks Road; they were later transferred to the adjacent but much larger Radcliffe Science Library, built to the designs of Thomas Graham Jackson, architect of the Examination Schools, in 1897–1901.

By the end of the nineteenth century, the Bodleian's book collection was growing by more than 30,000 volumes a year, and the number of books had reached the million mark by 1914. To provide extra storage space an underground book store was excavated beneath Radcliffe Square in 1909–12; it was at the time the largest such store in the world, and the first to use modern compact shelving. But with both readers and books inexorably increasing, the pressure on space once more became critical, leading some members of the university to propose moving the library to a more spacious site elsewhere, as was done in Cambridge when its new University Library was built in 1931–4. This did not happen, however, and in 1931 the decision was taken to build a new library, housing bookstacks for five million books, library departments and reading rooms, on a site occupied by a row of old timber houses on the north side of Broad Street. The new building went up to the designs of Sir Giles Gilbert Scott, architect of the Cambridge University Library, in 1937–40.

The building of the New Library allowed some rationalization of the older buildings to allow more space for the growing numbers of undergraduates, graduate students and visiting scholars. The former gallery on the top floor of the Schools Quadrangle had already become a reading room (the Upper Reading Room), and the former schools on the floor below, long used for book storage, now became the Lower Reading Room, leaving the ground floor for offices. In 1960–3 Duke Humfrey's Library underwent a major restoration, including the refacing of its decaying, blackened facades in Clipsham stone, along with those of Selden End and Arts End; the refacing of the rest of the Schools Quadrangle followed in 1964–8. In 1975 new office space was acquired in the Clarendon Building, built for the University Press in 1712–13, and occupying the crucial site between the Old and New Libraries. Thus the whole area between the Radcliffe Camera and the New Library – the historic core of the university – came into the hands of the Bodleian.

David Loggan engraving of the Old Schools Quadrangle.

The buildings of the Bodleian complex are linked by a series of enclosed spaces which form a public corridor known as the 'Pevsner Walk'. This view looks south through the arches of the Clarendon Building and Old Bodleian towards the Radcliffe Camera.

Exterior view of Sir Thomas Bodley's Library. This building extended Duke Humfrey's Library to create the Old Schools Quadrangle, using a Perpendicular Gothic style to blend as seamlessly as possible with the older building and the Divinity School.

Section of the Radcliffe Camera from James Gibbs' *Bibliotheca Radcliviana*, 1747.

A Section Shewing the Inside of the Library

An aerial view of the Bodleian complex in 1946, showing the Radcliffe Camera at the centre front, with the Old Bodleian and Clarendon Building sitting between it and the New Bodleian – which appears at the right of the picture. This photograph may have been taken at the official opening of the New Bodleian by King George VI, as large crowds can be seen gathering along Catte Street towards the new building.

Conserving Scott's Bodleian
Michael Morrison

I was approached by Oxford's university library service in February 2006 to complete a conservation statement for the New Bodleian against a background of potentially radical change in the operation of the libraries. The building was no longer serving its purpose adequately – crucially it was failing to provide suitable environmental conditions for the proper protection of the collection, and was being threatened with the loss of its status as a national archive. There seemed to be a good case for abandoning the building as a part of the library service. Given its Grade II-listed status it seemed highly unlikely that complete demolition of the building and redevelopment of this sensitive central Oxford site would be permitted and so it might be necessary to consider what new uses the building could be conveniently put to. The aim of the conservation statement was to analyse the New Bodleian in its then current state, in order to provide a better comprehension of the history, significance and vulnerability of the site. Such an understanding was intended to encourage proper upkeep and management of the building in the future as well as to consider what degree of alteration might be acceptable.

This was a building that I knew well from the exterior and felt no great affection for. A large and rather forbidding building occupying the corner of Parks Road and Broad Street, it did not offer any sort of welcome to the passing pedestrian. The style of the architecture – a bland mix of the vernacular touched with elements of both the beaux arts tradition and a hint of the modern movement – was not something to make one stop and ponder the provenance of the building. It was therefore a surprise to discover, as the inspection of the building and the archive progressed, that I was gradually falling for its charm and becoming an enthusiast for its special qualities. The far-from-expected conclusion of the study was that this was a fine building and that every effort should be made to retain it as part of the main library complex of the university.

The Bodleian Library's problems were those familiar to libraries everywhere – an ever-growing collection and the ever greater need for storage space. This was, and indeed still is, exacerbated at the Bodleian as it is one of the six libraries in the country which are entitled (not obliged, as is the British Library) to receive, under the Copyright Act of 1842, a copy of any book published in Great Britain. The history of the library from its beginnings is one of piecemeal expansion, building new wings or incorporating other buildings such as the Radcliffe Camera – which was built originally as a separate medical library and reading room. The most recent expansion of the library had been the construction, immediately preceding World War I, of the extensive two-storey underground bookstack between the Radcliffe Camera and the south wing of the Bodleian's Old Schools Quadrangle.

In 1925 Bodley's Librarian, Dr Arthur Ernest Cowley, informed Bodley's curators that the library would simply run out of space within the next ten years. One of the curators, Sir Michael Sadler, consequently drew up a pamphlet outlining five ways that the problem might be dealt with. His possible solutions ranged from discarding past accessions that were no longer seen as useful and reducing further additions to the collection, through to the more radical suggestions of a completely new building on the University Parks or outside Oxford altogether.

Original watercolour perspectives prepared by Giles Gilbert Scott's studio – now held in the Royal Institute of British Architects (RIBA) Library Drawings and Archives Collection at the Victoria and Albert Museum in London – showing views of the New Library from Trinity College gardens (above) and from Catte Street (below).

49

The general consensus of the University Council was that the Bodleian's associations with historic central Oxford should not be lost. Alterations to the existing library buildings were heartily unwelcome, and it was therefore decided that the construction of a new building within the city centre, which could accommodate the demand for more modern facilities, was the best course of action.

In 1926, the Rockefeller Foundation agreed to provide three-fifths of the cost of a new library, provided that the university would contribute the remainder. This was the catalyst for the creation of a 'Commission', under Sir Henry Miers, which was to visit modern university libraries in Europe and America, and to report on these with the intent of informing designs for the new library. In a report published in 1931, the Library Commission determined that the best course of action would be to abandon thoughts of a library and instead build a bookstack. The site chosen was opposite the Clarendon Building, to the north of Broad Street.

Following the appointment of Sir Giles Gilbert Scott as architect in June 1934, it was decided that the new building on the Broad Street site would be a book store and library extension capable of holding approximately 5,000,000 books, connected to the old Bodleian via a mechanical conveyor belt and pneumatic tube system. These decisions were influenced by extensive tours to European and American libraries, and indeed the concept for New Bodleian was very similar to an extension of the Library of Congress in Washington DC, USA. These tours were documented in detail at the time, with records currently held by the RIBA and within the Bodleian Library collections.

Along with the functional aspects of the building, other elements had to be considered in its design. City building regulations required a height restriction of 50 feet, and the site itself was limited to an acre. These limitations, combined with the desire to create a structure which was visually sympathetic to the surrounding historic environment, were a significant challenge for Scott.

In choosing Sir Giles Gilbert Scott as their architect for the new library building, the university was making a conservative choice. He was the son of George Gilbert Scott Junior and grandson of the eminent Victorian gothic revival architect Sir George Gilbert Scott – perhaps best remembered for St Pancras railway station. Giles Gilbert Scott had, astonishingly, won the competition for the new Liverpool Anglican Cathedral in 1903 when he was only twenty-two years old, and the completion of the cathedral was a project which would occupy him for the rest of his life. However, by 1934 Scott was fifty-four and very much at the heart of the architectural establishment. He had been president of the Architectural Association between 1920 and 1921 and was knighted in 1924. He received the RIBA's Royal Gold Medal in 1925 and in 1934, when he was appointed as architect for the New Bodleian, he was president of the RIBA. Apart from the cathedral in Liverpool, Scott is remembered for a series of iconic buildings: Battersea Power Station, Bankside Power Station (now the Tate Modern), and, most relevantly, Cambridge University Library.

The Bodleian Building Committee was established in June 1935. The main task of this planning sub-committee was to prepare the 'Instructions to the Architect', which were officially delivered on 15 June 1935. It would appear that Scott himself, as well as the newly appointed Bodley's Librarian Sir Edmund Craster, were closely involved with the production of this document, which is still held in the library's collections.

Scott's portfolio: (clockwise from top left) Anglican Cathedral, Liverpool; Battersea Power Station, London; Bankside Power Station (now Tate Modern), London; University Library, Cambridge.

Construction began in December 1936. A number of historic buildings belonging to the university on Broad Street and Parks Road were demolished. This was not an unusual occurrence in Oxford, where the university had previously taken down historic buildings on Broad Street to make way for the Indian Institute and its later extensions, as well as for Hertford College. A row of thirteen terraced houses dating from the first half of the seventeenth century were demolished on Broad Street. On Park Road, numbers two to four were demolished, along with St Stephen's House, an Anglican theological college and Ripon Hall. There were some good outcomes from this demolition. Dr William Pantin pioneered the techniques of above-ground archaeology to record the demolished buildings, and Bruce-Mitford of the Ashmolean Museum carried out one of England's first rescue excavations at the site. His studies resulted in the first complete 'modern' study of medieval pottery, and his chronological sequence of pottery for Oxford has been extended, but never challenged.

The foundation stone was laid by Queen Mary in June 1937 and construction was finally completed, to a cost of £379,300, in 1940, nine months after the start of World War II. Because of the war situation, the university was unable to open the building as a library directly after its completion, and it was used instead as a base for military operations for the remainder of the war. No obvious evidence of this military occupation remained in the building and, while it was not open for use, the library staff used the war years to transfer some 1.5 million books into the new bookstacks. The official opening by King George VI took place in October 1946. When he came to unlock the door of the Broad Street entrance, the key – designed by Scott himself – broke in its lock.

The finished building was a topic of heated debate. It was criticized and commended equally in all respects – from the choice of material to the layout and the exterior design. Most worrying was the underlying question of the building's capacity, which was highly debatable. The new stacks contained some 188 kilometres of shelving. Sir Ernest Cowley believed that this would provide for the needs of one hundred years, while Scott felt it sufficient for two hundred. In practice, it is now ninety years since Cowley brought the problem to the attention of the Bodley curators and seventy since the building opened for its proper use.

The librarian Craster described the New Bodleian project as being 'an experiment in working a new library building into an old historic framework'.[1] Scott's response to the challenge of the brief and the constricted site was to create a unique style which is an art deco/art moderne take on classical revivalism. The combined use of materials, styles, architectural features and design elements form a modern building in keeping with the style of its time, though touched rather heavily by the inspiration of the surrounding buildings – which range from medieval timber frames to the ornate classical revivalism of the Sheldonian Theatre and Clarendon Building. The *Architect and Building News* described the building in August 1940 as follows: 'The elevations are designed with due respect to the traditions that produced the surrounding old buildings, but no attempt has been made to ignore modern tendencies.'

The New Bodleian under construction: view south showing excavation beginning on site, with the Clarendon Building and Sheldonian Theatre beyond (top); and a view north from the Clarendon as the structural framework begins to take shape (bottom).

Construction progresses as the steelwork of the central stack is wrapped in three-storey perimeter block (top), and Broad Street is closed to traffic (bottom).

In 1940, Scott's completed building with its 'strangely mixed style of detail' had extensive coverage in the architectural press. Shown here are extracts of articles from *The Architect and Building News* (top) and *The Architectural Review* (bottom).

BODLEIAN LIBRARY ~ OXFORD.

Design for proposed Presentation Key.

Full-size.

MAY 1946.

SIR GILES GILBERT SCOTT O.M. R.A.
3. FIELD COURT. GRAY'S INN. W.C.1.

Scott's attention to detail even extended to the ceremonial key used (unsuccessfully) by King George VI to open the building.

This contemporary photograph shows huge crowds gathered to witness the opening of the building and the accompanying academic and regal pageantry.

Unfortunately, as the king came to unlock the door with Scott's ceremonial key, it broke in the lock.

Arguments over the quality of the design have continued to the present day. The conservation plan prepared in 2000 stated that, 'The New Bodleian suffers from not having a distinctive architectural style – it is neither evocative of the Oxford college nor can it be described as modern.'[2] The document continues to speculate on the stylistic in Scott but this seems to be rather irrelevant. Scott's style was fully developed by this point in his career and it seems probable that he took a personal hand in the design – he was certainly involved in the tours of the European and American libraries and much involved in correspondence over the developing scheme. The restrained architectural treatment blends simplified classical detail with contemporary references, something that seems to be very much Scott's own work.

It must be recognized that the New Bodleian was designed primarily as a bookstack and secondarily as a library. This was due in large part to the reorganization of the whole Bodleian complex, with books being relocated from the Old Bodleian to the New. The freeing up of space allowed the Old Bodleian to function almost entirely as reading rooms, thus requiring the major function of the New Bodleian to be the housing of books.

Early designs suggested a double stack system, with a stack each for the Rhodes and Taylor Collections. However, when the final design was approved, it was for a single central bookstack. The eleven-storey, 78-foot high stack was masked by a three-storey 'screen' of perimeter accommodation, one room deep, separated from the stack itself by a connecting corridor. Each floor of the stack had a height of either 7'6" or 8', depending on whether the floor of the stack needed to correspond with the levels of the double-height perimeter spaces. The three lowest basement floors spread across the entirety of the site, housing more bookstacks together with plant room space and the operating system for the book conveyor and pneumatic tube system. At the lowest level was the entrance to a tunnel, containing the conveyor, which led across to the book store below the Radcliffe Camera. Except for the three top levels, which were exposed on all sides to the exterior, the stacks were lit and ventilated entirely by artificial means.

The central stack concept was heavily influenced by the libraries visited by Scott and Craster on their extensive European and American tours early in the development of the design. As Craster makes clear in a letter to the Registrar in 1935:

My Curators have under consideration a proposal (based on conclusions which I have drawn from my American tour) for the planning of the new library building on Broad Street as a solid stack.[3]

The decision to include a book conveyor and pneumatic tubing system was also a direct result of the study tours, particularly the inspection of such systems at the State Library in Berlin, and also from viewing the innovative delivery systems being pioneered in America. Yale Sterling Memorial and Columbia University Library were both arranged as a central stack with pneumatic tube system and mechanical conveyor (though in both libraries these systems have been replaced in recent renovations). The New Bodleian is especially comparable to the annexe to the Library of Congress in Washington DC, which was designed as a large book storage facility which communicates with the main library across a major roadway by way of an underground tunnel and mechanical book conveyor.

Scott's original drawings – now held in the RIBA archive – combine elevations, sections and plans on a single sheet, each element cleverly interlinked to give a three-dimensional impression of the building. Shown here is the formal entrance vestibule in the south-east corner of the building.

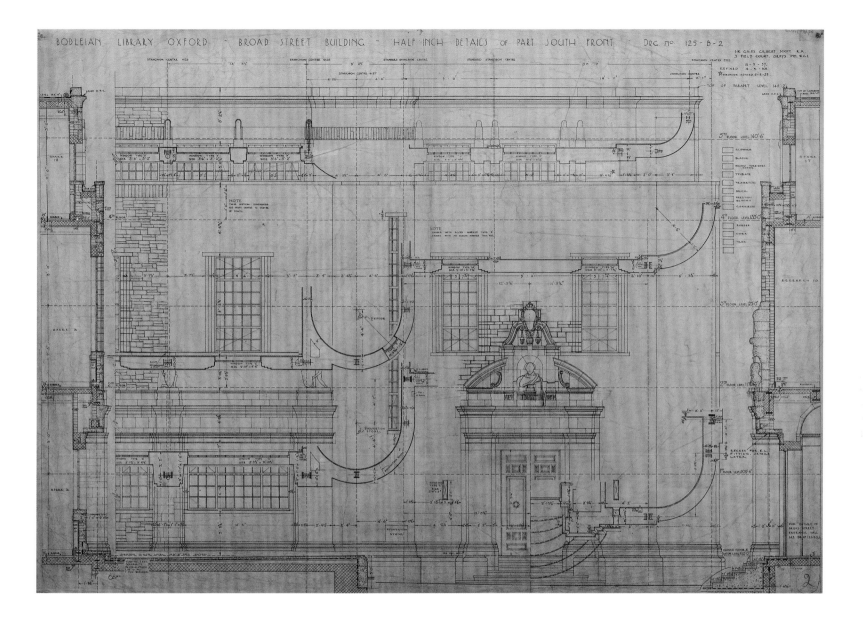

While Scott designed the building, and therefore the layout and placement of rooms, it is known that the storage expert Roneo was responsible for the actual design of the bookstack. Roneo supplied everything 'from shelving, map cases and catalogue cases to furniture, clocks, the book elevator and the casing to the conveyor and pneumatic tubes'.[4] The shelving system was, in effect, the structure of the central stack, the relatively lightweight steel frame providing the support for the kilometres of bookshelves and also the floors. The masonry simply provided an outer weatherproof skin. The system was a modern variant of the cast iron bookstacks of many nineteenth-century libraries and did provide an economical way of supporting the bookshelves. However, it also created a very inflexible overall layout – with one section of the stack looking much like every other. This was not so much of a problem when the stack was being accessed only by the librarians – who could be expected to become familiar with the way around – but it made it a very perplexing and confusing space for anyone else who had to access the area. Similarly, it was not a space that could sensibly accommodate free access by readers. The limited artificial ventilation was incapable of producing anything approaching the stable conditions required by a modern archive, and the very limited head heights and the inflexibility of the steel frame made the fitting of a new air-conditioning system more or less impossible.

The decision to build the New Bodleian as a book store for the reading rooms in the old library areas meant that it was necessary for a connection to exist between the Old and New Bodleian. This took the form of the book conveyor and pneumatic tubing system, both of which led from the underground bookstack of the new building into the Old Bodleian via a tunnel under Broad Street. While the mechanics of the conveyor were located at the lowest level of the building, each floor of the stack had a sorting area where orders could be received, filled and sent out, and returned books could be distributed back to their correct resting place. If books were too large to be transported using this system, they would be taken on a trolley, via the tunnel, to their final destination. The conveyor system was designed and installed by

Sovex,[5] a company that still exists as part of Conveyors International and which still makes book conveyors. Sovex were installing similar conveyors in the 1930s in many post office sorting centres and also in the British Library and Glasgow Public Library.

The vacuum tube system was designed and installed by the Lamson[6] engineering company. This system was also still operating in 2006 using the original motor, pumps, tubing and stations – although it had largely been superseded by email. The system was designed to convey the request slips from the reading rooms to the appropriate base stations in the stacks to allow books to be loaded onto the conveyors for delivery. The Lamson Company still exists and is still involved in installing vacuum systems. The system was widely used at the time it was installed in the New Bodleian for inconspicuously removing cash from tills in shops and supermarkets, and this is still its primary use.

Scott's original drawing for a stack conveyor station, from which books were removed from the stack and delivered to the reading rooms, and returned books were received and replaced within the stack.

A contemporary photograph shows the conveyor station as built.

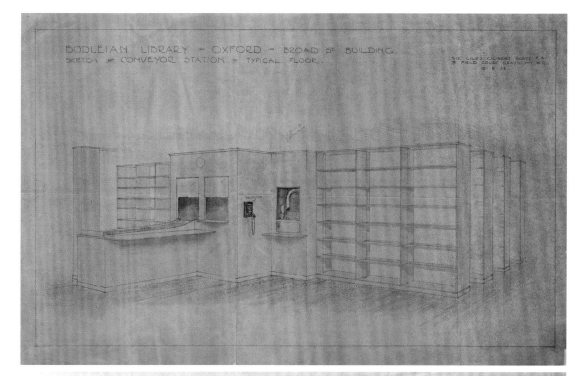

BODLEIAN LIBRARY ~ OXFORD ~ BROAD ST BUILDING.
SKETCH OF CONVEYOR STATION ~ TYPICAL FLOOR.

SIR GILES GILBERT SCOTT R.A.
3 FIELD COURT GRAYS INN W.C.

While the internal layout of the bookstacks was quite inflexible due to the steel support structure, the surrounding ground-to-second floor levels were intended by Scott to be flexible – not least as they might be needed for conversion for additional stack space in the future. The problems of lack of storage space have, of course, been addressed since by the provision of off-site storage, yet the perimeter rooms have indeed been partitioned off and altered in order to accommodate more offices and administration spaces. This three-storey screen effectively masked the stacks from the exterior, wrapping completely around them. Inside, the offices and reading rooms were placed on the external faces of the building and lit by large aluminium windows. They were reached by an eight-foot wide corridor between the ante rooms and the central stack. The outer rooms and the corridor were light and spacious, the floor to ceiling height occupying the space equivalent to two floors of the stack. By contrast the stack spaces were dark and cramped.

Various minor alterations have taken place throughout the life of the Bodleian. These have been due to changing functions in certain areas of the building, necessitating the creation of additional rooms through the partitioning mentioned above. Other minor changes to the interior have included the updating of finishes and light fittings. The most significant change, though, was the construction of the south-facing extension at roof level to house the Indian Institute Library. This was built between 1966 and 1969 to the designs of Robert Potter, after the old Indian Institute building (1896, Basil Champneys) was appropriated by the university for use as offices (now the History Faculty). This penthouse addition to New Bodleian was controversial, as it was highly visible at street level and added nothing to the character or significance of Scott's design, and it is one of the bonuses of the present-day scheme that this has been removed. However, while changes have been made to the outer rooms, the bookstack itself has remained almost entirely unchanged – due no doubt to the inflexible nature of its construction.

One of the most remarkable features of the building was in Scott's attention to detail. He specified high-quality materials for both public and private spaces and, as well as the architectural detailing of the structure of the building, also gave a great deal of attention to the design of the interior fittings. Skirtings, cornices, architraves, doors and door furniture were all carefully detailed by the architect. Much of the original furniture and light fittings were designed by Scott for particular spaces. This included reading tables and chairs, of which there are many examples of the same design, and also 'one off' pieces, such as an impressive art-deco style conference table with inlaid burl veneer and a secretary's desk of similar style, both of which still survive.

Many of the original design drawings for the furniture and ironmongery survive in the Bodleian archive. It must be highly unusual for any building to remain so unchanged over a period of sixty years – and even more so for the original uses to be much the same. The generation of scholars using the library in the early 2000s sat in the same chairs and at the same desks as the first users of the building in the 1940s. The survival of so much of the furniture and of the original fittings made this a special building and an especially good example of Scott's work.

Despite my initial feelings of indifference towards the building, by the time the conservation statement was complete I had come to regard Scott's design as a splendid and ingenious way to fit an enormous amount of storage onto a difficult site. The most significant aspect of the building remained that identified by Sir Michael Sadler in 1925:

Whatever is done, Bodley's end of the ancient Library together with Duke Humfrey's Library and the Selden End should be inviolate. To destroy their associations with the Bodleian would be vandalism.[7]

Internal views of the New Bodleian on completion: (clockwise from top left) shelving within the bookstack; bronze screens to the PPE Catalogue Room (now the Mackerras Reading Room); the stone-veneered ceremonial entrance off Broad Street; stairs at the north end of the east corridor.

The reasoning still held good that to remove the library or a part of the library to a new site would be to rip the heart out of the institution which is the centre of the university. Efficient new systems and good transport meant that it was entirely possible to have a bookstack off site but the library itself, together with the special collections and the most regularly used books, needed to remain together in the centre of Oxford. Clearly the New Bodleian, which had served so well as a bookstack for sixty years, was no longer fit for purpose. The environmental conditions needed to be improved, the stacks needed to be turned into shelving accessible to readers, and the building needed to be made more open and welcoming to visitors. The challenge was how to achieve this without destroying the character of Scott's building. This seems to have been brilliantly achieved by WilkinsonEyre. The external character of Scott's building remains virtually unchanged apart from the beneficial removal of the 1960 extension and the opening up of the new south doors. The solid stone masonry of the south elevation at street level and the raised paved area keeping passers-by away was one of the building's more forbidding aspects. Opening these up has transformed the way the building feels in the street, while internally, the best of Scott's carefully designed rooms have been retained and it is exceptionally pleasing to see that scholars will continue to sit at the same chairs and desks that Scott designed.

[1] E. Craster, *The Bodleian Library Extension Scheme*, Manchester, 1941.
[2] TfT Cultural Heritage, *The Bodleian Library Oxford – Conservation Plan*, 2000.
[3] Copy of letter from Librarian to Registrar, 23 February 1935. RIBA SCGG/104/1-2.
[4] S. Aird, *University of Oxford New Bodleian Library Design Concept History* (unpublished), 2005.
[5] Taken from *The Architect & Building News*, 30 August 1940.
[6] Ibid.
[7] Proofs of *The Future of the Bodleian*, 1926. Bodleian Library collection Johnson d.4736.

External views of the completed building: looking west down Broad Street, showing the south facade and the steps of the Clarendon Building opposite (top); and, turning slightly towards the north, a view of the south-east entrance during the early 1960s.

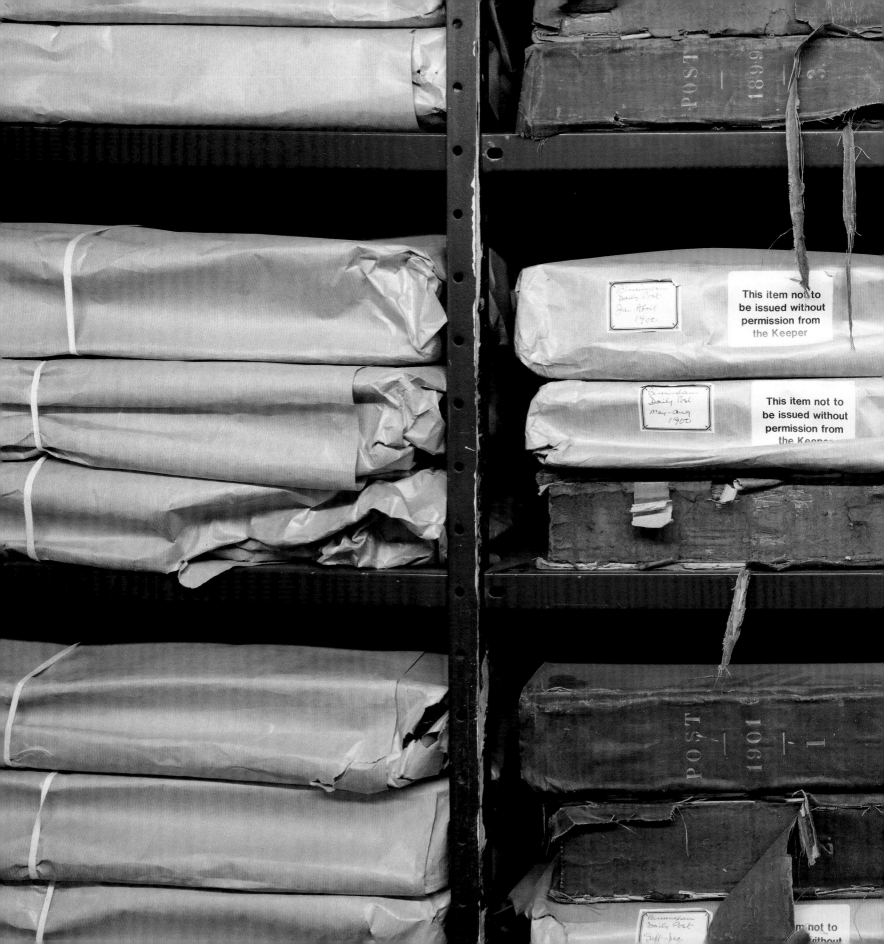

The vision

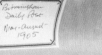

A new vision for the Bodleian
Richard Ovenden

The New Bodleian Library was built in the late 1930s and completed in 1940 to a brief and design which were essentially complete by 1937. Although the New Bodleian had been planned to serve the university's needs for the following century, by the late 1990s it was clear that the academic and operational context which allowed H.H.E. Craster and Giles Gilbert Scott to bring forward and conceive this radical building had changed so dramatically that a rethink was required.

The principal impetus for this rethink was preservation. The method of construction of the New Bodleian – based around a large and complex unprotected steel frame with concrete infills – held a significant conceptual flaw. With the content of the New Bodleian largely consisting of highly combustible materials – chiefly paper, of course – any fire which might ignite inside the library would rapidly take hold (as the building held no fire suppression system as part of its basic infrastructure), would swiftly pass through the floors of the building and reach a temperature quite quickly which would cause the steel frame to buckle and the building to collapse.

Fire is chief among the threats which librarians fear most. The destruction of the library of Alexandria is one of the most famous episodes in intellectual history as so much knowledge from the ancient world was irretrievably lost in it. The Bodleian's own oath, dating from 1602 and still in daily use, requires all new readers to swear that they will not 'kindle fire nor flame in the library'. By the late 1990s, major fires in Los Angeles, St Petersburg and Norwich had highlighted the risks of uncontrollable fire in a library. A number of professional investigations and consultancy reports were commissioned by the Bodleian to discover the level of risk posed by the state of the stacks in the New Bodleian, and this prompted Bodley's Librarian, Dr Reg Carr, to raise the issue

formally within the university's governing structures.

At the same time as these concerns were being investigated and were becoming better understood within the Bodleian and the broader university, a space crisis was once again becoming apparent within the Bodleian's estate. As a major collecting institution, with the benefit of legal deposit, as well as making significant purchases of new publications from around the world and the occasional major acquisition of archival collections, the Bodleian has throughout its 400-year history built its collections faster than it has built spaces to store them. By 2003 the Bodleian's existing off-site storage facility at Nuneham Courtenay was close to capacity, and the New Bodleian building had been filled up to beyond safe capacity. In early 2004 planning permission for a new storage module at Nuneham Courtenay was refused by Oxford City Council, prompting a crisis which was compounded by an inspection of the New Bodleian stacks which found that the over-filling of the stacks there had caused serious health and safety problems. The conclusion was that collections stored there had to be moved out rapidly, and that a fundamental re-think of the library's storage strategy was required.

The immediate needs for storage were met by purchasing commercial storage capacity at Deepstore's facility in Cheshire: a salt-mine converted for mixed storage which began to be used by the Bodleian in 2004 (it had been used by The National Archives and by the John Rylands Library of the University of Manchester before, proving its worth). The longer-term solution that was rapidly developed was the creation of a single BS 5454 compliant facility, modelled on the high-bay depositories developed in the US. An initial site was found close to Oxford's city centre, but planning issues proved impossible to surmount – even after protracted efforts – and the Bodleian's own Book Storage Facility

(BSF) was eventually constructed in South Marston, 25 miles to the west of the Bodleian. It was completed in September 2010 and allowed the Bodleian to move out of its Nuneham Courtenay facility, the commercial storage in Cheshire, and various other storage areas in central Oxford. Most importantly it provided a location for the safe decant of the contents of the New Bodleian, while that building was being renovated. The Book Storage Facility eventually cost £26 million, part of which was the cost of temporary storage for the New Bodleian – which was invested in the more permanent infrastructure of the BSF.

The combined needs for overhauling the preservation infrastructure of the New Bodleian and providing more space prompted the Bodleian to use the opportunity of the 400th anniversary of its founding to launch a £40 million campaign to renovate the building. This campaign focused almost exclusively on the essential issues of fire safety, air handling (to provide stable temperature and relative humidity for the collections) as well as improved shelving. Compliance with the British Standard BS 5454: 2000 was central to this strategy. The scheme was backed by a £10 million pledge from the university, but by the middle of 2004 had raised only a few million pounds and had generated no significant leads. The feedback from potential supporters was that the core infrastructure of such a key building for the university ought to be funded by the university itself.

During 2004–5, led by Oxford's new vice chancellor, John Hood, the Bodleian team, under Reg Carr's leadership as Bodley's Librarian, re-evaluated the campaign, including the 'case for support'. Also brought into this picture was the very closely related issue of space, the lack of which was by now becoming urgent, as the costs of Deepstore were increasing with every additional book placed there for storage.

Another factor which was a strong influence at this point was the relationship between the Bodleian and the National Archives (TNA) Advisory Service, which had inherited responsibilities from the old Historic Manuscripts Commission (HMC) for evaluating the ability of repositories to hold public records under the terms of the 1958 Public Records Act. The quinquennial inspections which the HMC and TNA staff had made to the Bodleian from the 1990s onwards had evaluated the Bodleian against BS 5454, and the TNA's own Standard for Record Repositories. These standards had long been regarded as sensible minimum requirements for the good practice of keeping archival and manuscript collections (and by analogy rare book and other special collections), but it became increasingly clear to Bodleian staff that without a major renovation to the New Bodleian and a solution to the space crisis, there was a real risk of the Bodleian's ability to hold records under the 1958 act being withdrawn.

There were also new scholarly imperatives to consider in the planning for the renovation of the New Bodleian. Libraries have always been concerned with both holding material and making it available, chiefly through reading rooms. But through the 1990s a number of libraries had begun to be interested in hosting alternative kinds of engagement with their collections other than quiet solitary study in reading rooms. The ability for small groups of people to collectively view and discuss an individual rare book or manuscript (or indeed groups of collection items) in a teaching situation is the most obvious example of how the changing use of collections was driving changing demands of space, but the ability to present materials as part of a masterclass or public lecture was also beginning to be prevalent. Some special collections libraries, like the Bodleian, with large and very broadly based holdings, can support a wide variety of subjects in teaching terms, and so some libraries had, by the late twentieth and early twenty-first centuries, begun to develop suites of seminar rooms and to add small lecture theatres to their buildings, to accommodate the demand in both size and frequency of use. Such uses were not just confined to teaching and research situations, but also to add value to exhibitions and other activities designed to widen access to the collections.

Exhibitions were in fact another key factor for change in the thinking behind the New Bodleian redevelopment. The Bodleian had been an exhibiting institution for many years, with the first vitrine being installed in the library in the late eighteenth century. Throughout the twentieth century, exhibition cases had been installed in the Divinity Schools, where generations of undergraduates and others had enjoyed their contents (including the poet Andrew Motion, who saw the Shelley notebooks there, inspiring him towards poetry himself). By the 1990s, the conservation issues relating to exhibitions had become better known and the Bodleian refitted one of the rooms in the Old Schools Quadrangle to be a better equipped exhibition room, with some limited environmental controls, improved lighting and more secure cases. But the room was comparatively small, and being located in one of the most historic buildings in the country, the ability to change and adapt the space to suit the needs of a state-of-the-art exhibition gallery were severely constrained. In 2004, the Bodleian acquired the archives of Mary Shelley and her parents Mary Wollstonecraft and William Godwin. This archive – which included the manuscript of *Frankenstein* as one of the star items – was acquired with a major grant (of £3 million) from the National Heritage Memorial Fund, and this public funding came with expectations of public access. A visit to the Bodleian from the then Chairman of the Fund, Dame Liz Forgan, in 2005 made it clear that unless the library was able to dramatically improve its

exhibition facilities and show more of the materials acquired through public funding, future grants would be jeopardized.

Exhibitions were themselves also changing beyond merely the expectations of public funding bodies. The Bodleian's own strategy had been developing to allow greater engagement between the public and the research community in Oxford, through its collections. A series of exhibitions including 'The Book of Curiosities' in 2005, 'Citizen Milton' in 2008 and 'Shelley's Ghost' in 2010 showed how large audiences could be engaged with major scholarly projects, led by Oxford academics. Visitors to Bodleian exhibitions, rather than being put off by their engagement with challenging academic research, had increased substantially, from an average of 35,000 per year in 2003 to over 150,000 for the 2013–14 academic year. In 2013, the summer exhibition alone received over 100,000 visitors.

A similar change was also happening in the realm of the practice and behaviour of academics around library support for teaching and research. With rich and diverse primary source research collections at their disposal, Oxford academics throughout the 1990s and 2000s were increasingly interested in bringing students into close contact with special collections items. With the Bodleian buildings not having been designed to support teaching activity of this kind, and with demand growing, it became clear that new facilities were needed to support teaching with special collections: small-scale seminar activity in rooms that provided BS 5454 standard-compliant temperature and relative humidity controls, but which were also secure and close to the holding areas for fetched materials. In addition, a masterclass programme developed by the Bodleian's Centre for the Study of the Book had also shown a significant demand for teaching and research engagement with graduate students in key disciplines.

A technology-rich lecture theatre was also added to the list of desirable new features at this point in order to accommodate this graduate-level activity, but also to allow for functions put on by the Friends of the Bodleian to take place in a comfortable and well-equipped lecture space which was also a BS 5454 compliant environment. By 2013 'Wider Engagement with Society' had become one of the core elements of the university's Strategic Plan, which the Bodleian's own strategy and its now well-advanced plans for the renovation of the New Bodleian were therefore well placed to support.

As the planning for the New Bodleian progressed, the impact of technology on library operations also became more apparent. One immediate need was the provision of a high-quality digital imaging facility in the building, to allow for the often fragile and vulnerable special collections items to be scanned in situ. Such a facility also entailed the creation of a suitable server room and high-bandwidth internet connection to allow the movement of high-resolution digital imagery. With consistent numbers of digital imaging projects undertaken by the Bodleian from the mid-1990s onwards, the arrival of digitally intensive scholarship was a natural step forward. With the provision of ultra-high-resolution screens, the availability of specialist software to manipulate digital images, and the advances in geo-spatial software and digital mapping, the need for a facility (based around the more traditional library feature of a reading room) also became apparent. The Bodleian's Map Room had become very advanced in its use and instructional services in digital mapping, and this requirement led the way in the conception of a 'Digital Media Centre' which would provide readers with access to the latest hardware and software to enable digital scholarship, and also to specialist support from technically capable library staff.

If the major drivers for the renovation were the need to overhaul the preservation infrastructure of the building, and to provide improved services for scholars using the Bodleian's special collections, then the needs of staff were not overlooked either. In particular the Bodleian's Department of Conservation and Collections Care had previously been split between four different buildings in nine separate locations, where it was hard for specialist conservators to work in teams and to configure ways of working to suit different types of collections. The development of an integrated conservation centre was therefore a high-demand item within the planning requirements. Also on this list were improved facilities for the curatorial staff of the Department of Special Collections in order to foster exactly the same kind of synergistic working that was recognized as necessary for conservation. In addition, it was also recognized that the Bodleian would greatly benefit from the closer working of specialists in conservation and curators in Special Collections. Being co-located in the same building would greatly enhance this operational change, but so too would a dedicated space in the building where collaborative project work involving staff from both departments could take place. Within the stacks as well, new facilities were identified: a cold-store for photographic collections; a quarantine room, where newly acquired collections could be safely checked for insect and microbial infestation before being brought into the stacks; and an area for the appraisal of large archival collections.

One further aspect of the Bodleian's special collections which was being considered at the start of the project related to visiting scholars. The Bodleian has never had any difficulty in attracting scholars from other institutions. Since the opening of the Bodleian Library in 1602, scholars with no direct affiliation with the University of Oxford have visited the library in order to consult its collections, interact with other scholars there, or work with the staff of the library. The importance of the Bodleian to visiting scholars from the US in the 1930s was a key factor in the massive benefaction from the Rockefeller Foundation that provided three-fifths of the cost of the New Bodleian building. By the 1990s many US special collections libraries – such as the Beinecke at Yale, the Houghton at Harvard and the Folger in Washington DC – were providing endowed funds to support scholars wishing to consult their collections. In 2004–5 the Bodleian acquired the archive of Marconi plc, and with it philanthropic funds were donated to support scholars from outside Oxford to come and consult this key collection for the history of science and communication. This prompted consideration of a facility which could accommodate and organize a series of visiting fellowships, based around areas of pre-eminent strength in the collections. This would enable the best scholars around the world to compete for funds to study the Bodleian's collections in a dedicated facility, with excellent access to library staff, but where, in return, they would be asked to contribute back to the research culture of the university through, for example, teaching graduate students, giving a seminar paper to one of the existing seminar series, or a public lecture. By 2014 the Bodleian had sixteen fellowships either endowed or funded on an annual basis by learned societies, foundations or individuals.

With these practical, operational and strategic drivers aligned, the Bodleian was able, through a series of proposal documents, to attain the support of the university to progress through the standard RIBA design cycle and to advance the scheme. Feasibility was undertaken by a local firm of architects, Berman Guedes Stretton, and this led to a formal architectural competition in 2006 which was won by WilkinsonEyre. At the same time that the scheme moved forward from 2006, on to the completion of the design in 2010, the BSF was also progressed. It was moved from its original planned site on the Osney Mead Industrial Estate to a new site acquired by the university at South Marston, just to the east of Swindon. The new facility was designed and built between 2008 and 2010, with the first volumes being ingested in November 2010. By 2014, the BSF held over 7.5 million printed volumes and 1.5 million maps, and had 10 kilometres of manuscripts and archives. This allowed for the safe temporary storage of the special collections housed in the New Bodleian.

As the estates plan came together, so too did the fundraising. An approach was made to the Delegates of Oxford University Press (OUP) to provide a matched-funding proposition to put to major philanthropic prospects. The OUP secured £25 million for this purpose, based on the need for the university to upgrade the core building infrastructure, a requirement which the 2002 campaign had floundered on. With a serious matched-funding proposition, conversations were entered into with the Garfield Weston Foundation in 2006, and in 2008 they made their first payment towards a £25 million gift which resulted in the university agreeing to name the refurbished New Bodleian as 'The Weston Library of the Bodleian Libraries' on its completion. But the Garfield Weston Foundation gift was not the first major donation to the project. This was provided in March 2008 from Julian 'Toby' Blackwell, whose leadership gift of £5 million in that year started the public phase of the campaign (which at that point aimed at reaching £76.5 million). The Blackwell Gift would be recognized by naming the main grand entrance hall of the building after the family and the bookselling business that has been such a close friend, neighbour and partner through its lifetime of 130 years on Broad Street.

Other generous gifts soon followed: from the Polonsky Foundation; George Mallinckrodt; Joseph Sassoon; Doug Smith; Barrie and Deedee Wigmore; George and Charles David; Dr Lee Seng Tee; the Helen Hamlyn Trust; Antonio Bonchristiano; André Stern; Giancarlo Garuti; Dr Ebadolla Bahari; from Emerson, in honour of Sir Robert Horton; the Dunard Fund; and from numerous other donors.

The academic context in which the New Bodleian was conceived had changed dramatically by 2005. The University of Oxford was much larger and more research intensive than it had been in the 1930s, and the same was true of the broader academic climate across the globe. The Bodleian too had grown much faster than Craster and Scott had predicted in the 1930s, both in terms of the collections and in the size and shape of the organization.

What also had changed was the approach to the building itself. Designed pragmatically by Scott to be flexible in its future use in the perimeter parts of the structure above ground, the central stack tower and basement storage vaults were in fact designed by shelving specialists Roneo and were the inherent cause of the problems with the building infrastructure. In 2002, anticipating an architectural intervention in the building, the New Bodleian was Grade II listed at the behest of the Twentieth Century Society, thus placing constraints on any future building project. This move had been welcomed by the Bodleian – the institution that had commissioned the building in the 1930s was naturally concerned to ensure the preservation of its most significant heritage features, whilst also recognizing that in order to continue to function well as a library building, major changes were required. In 2005, the library commissioned a major conservation heritage survey of the building and its contents, from Purcell Miller Tritton Architects. This survey was given to WilkinsonEyre at the start of

their commission so that the heritage component of the renovation was informed, from the outset, by a detailed analysis of the original building and its contents.

The idea for the Weston Library was therefore borne out of the changing shape of the Bodleian Library as a whole. The Bodleian, by the early twenty-first century, was bigger and more research intensive than Sir Edmund Craster and Giles Gilbert Scott had predicted in the mid-1930s, and the university and the wider world of scholarship were also larger and more demanding than they were in the days of Craster and Scott. The technical standards that guide the world of libraries and archives had become better known and more developed than eighty years before, and the technologies to deliver them now existed, allowing the library to be compliant. Perhaps the biggest change was the desire of the University of Oxford – and its great research library – to engage with the broader public. This desire was present in Scott's mind when he designed the New Bodleian, but it would be the next millennium before the vision was put into reality.

Making the move
Toby Kirtley

The original refurbishment project was brought about by a fire safety report commissioned from Arup in 1998 which said there was a one in three chance of the whole building burning down if there was a fire. So the New Bodleian, and its need for a better fire infrastructure, became the centrepiece of the Bodleian's Capital Campaign. Although improving the fire infrastructure was necessary, it was also very expensive and would have delivered very little outside of the internal engineering of the building, so it didn't turn out to be a very attractive project for fundraising. Instead we took a wider view, looking at how we could improve conditions for storage but also increase public engagement and research facilities and this led to the appointment of WilkinsonEyre in 2006 as architects.

As estates project officer, I sit between the Bodleian (who I represent as 'tenant') and the estates and consultant teams. My role went right from building the business case and vision for the project, through to developing the brief, looking at space and occupancy levels, describing our work processes, and then the implementation and decant.

The Bodleian did a project before WilkinsonEyre's appointment which investigated the possibility of doing the work a floor at a time. But we soon realized we had to empty the building, and that meant that the decant was split into two parts – one to do with the housing of the staff and one to do with the housing of the collections.

Housing the New Bodleian staff meant finding space for the readers too. We closed the building, but we didn't close down our services. The reading room was moved to the Radcliffe Science Library, but staff had to be moved wherever space could be found. Some went to Osney Mead, and some of our departments now have that as their permanent home.

The Bodleian is concerned with forty-three libraries across Oxford. All of these had developed haphazardly over time, but in 2000 they were brought together under the umbrella of Oxford University Library Service. There was a realization that we could offer a far more co-ordinated service this way, and also that we could undertake a strategy of rationalization – removing duplications of stock and staffing across the collections, bringing every building under the same opening hours and so on. We had

growing collections in various buildings across the city, so some lower-use material was occupying prime real estate in the city centre, when actually it could easily have been kept further away off site.

There was a strong case for a high-capacity store. Although we had a low-density bookstore off site at Nuneham Courtenay, it couldn't keep up with demand, and there were constraints to the site so it couldn't be expanded. In 2003, we went on tour to the US to look at reference libraries, some of which had robot retrieval, and as a result we built the Swindon store in 2010, which has capacity for 9 million volumes. There, we've got a semi-automated, high bay book storage facility. It follows the model we saw at Harvard, where everything is kept in archival trays and then forklifts are used to take the trays to the shelves.

As soon as it was built, we started filling it, because by that time we had to start emptying the New Bodleian stacks. Our enabling work involved the decant of 17 kilometres of shelving, which was a huge, multi-million pound operation.

Before then we didn't have a complete grip on what we had – it was necessary that we identify and systemize the stock as we moved it to Swindon so that future retrieval would be possible – so a huge workforce was needed to barcode and catalogue the books. It was a massive logistical challenge: the books had to be transferred by road and then ingested into the Swindon store in archival trays.

If the decant of the collections was about logistics, the decant of staff during the project was about organizational change. By starting afresh we've been able to solve problems around adjacencies and communication between the various departments. In many ways the New Bodleian was a time capsule, but it's as if we've all had a new lease of life. Many of our traditions had emotional value – but they weren't necessarily contributing to our success as a modern research library. Were we discharging our duty to the British public before? Were we really facing the public at all? The traditions got in the way. Emptying the building completely gave us a chance to think again.

Photographs taken during the move illustrate the gargantuan task of moving 70 kilometres of books and objects, as well as furniture, equipment and staff – the biggest book move in the Bodleian's history. As the New Bodleian's stacks were emptied, many volumes were transported to a new storage facility near Swindon to be ingested there, while certain special collections were kept in Oxford at the Radcliffe Science Library.

The new Book Storage Facility (BSF) at Swindon has 230 kilometres of shelving, stacked at high density to provide the equivalent shelf surface area of 16.5 football pitches. Volumes are stored in specially designed, bar-coded storage trays and archive boxes, allowing the contents of the library to be fully digitized, and maps in special aisles of map cabinets.

The design

Facing up to Wren and Hawksmoor
Jim Eyre

The New Bodleian (now the Weston Library), as designed by Giles Gilbert Scott, is barely attached to the core Bodleian Library buildings. Just opposite is Nicholas Hawksmoor's confident and dynamic Clarendon Building, and neighbouring that, the radiused form of Christopher Wren's Sheldonian Theatre. Unlike them, Scott's building lies just outside the line of the old city wall, and perhaps this too contributes to the perception that it is not quite attached to the complex of buildings that make up one of the most remarkable sequences of urban spaces in the world. The Old Schools Quadrangle is the historical heart of the university and, with all the wonderful buildings that surround it, an architectural tour de force. James Gibb's Radcliffe Camera is the dominant landmark of the sequence and, with its height, circular form and more open setting, claims the centre of gravity of the complex. Many of the famous colleges surround these university buildings: Wadham, Hertford, All Soul's, Brasenose, Exeter and Trinity Colleges are but a stone's throw away and the little 'bridge of sighs' over New College Lane yet another delight.

It was back in 2006 that I started to think about the New Bodleian. While acknowledging that the core purpose of the project was of course the upgrading of its book storage and the creation of a special collections research library with facilities for public engagement, it was nevertheless the physical context of the building that initially generated inspiration for our design – and with it the idea of opening up the southern elevation at ground floor level. Inevitably I also recognized the heavy responsibility of intervening architecturally in so important a location. Standing at certain points in Catte Street, all one can see is buildings in warm, honeyed stone hewn from the quarries that surround the city. Scott's building is of the same stone and stands to the north of the main Bodleian group, with a deceptively shy presence on Broad Street. It is listed but not necessarily loved. Amusing remarks about the building from the past are often regaled: it is likened to appearing at a black tie event in a tweed dinner suit or, more bluntly, as having the appearance of a municipal swimming pool. However, as I got to know the building its finer qualities soon became apparent. It does not help that the building ambiguously turns away from the Bodleian complex, forcing

Competition sketch, diagram and drawing showing routes and connecting axes through the Bodleian complex. The complex includes the Old Bodleian libraries around the Old Schools Quadrangle, the Radcliffe Camera to the south, and Hawksmoor's Clarendon Building and Scott's New Bodleian Library to the north. Together with Wren's Sheldonian Theatre and St Mary's Church, these buildings form the physical and symbolic heart of the university, and a dramatic urban set-piece.

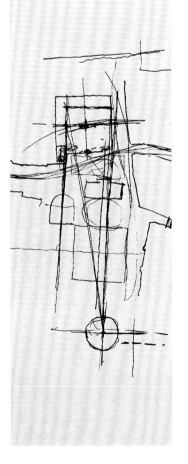

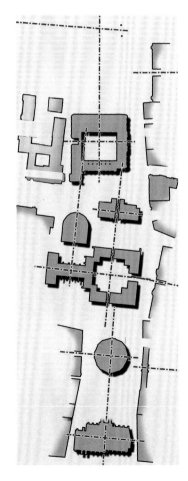

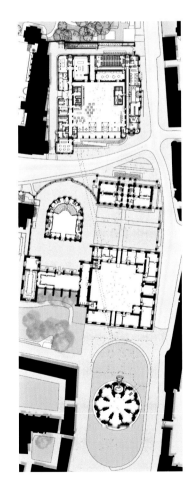

Scott's 1930s model of the Bodleian complex (top), and WilkinsonEyre's similar contextual model (below), made in 2007.

The New Bodleian sits at one end of the Pevsner Walk and, although it was never intended to be a public entrance, the King George VI door at its south-east corner is placed on axis with the sequence of connecting archways.

readers to enter from Parks Road. And, although Scott presented a considered, well-proportioned elevation to Broad Street, this was marred at ground level by a curious protruding plinth and a range of windows with high cills. This combination serves only to defy any desire to enter, thereby usurping many of the architecture's otherwise neighbourly qualities. Conceived in another era, primarily as overflow book storage for the reading rooms over the Old Quad and beyond, perhaps its ambivalent status was understandable. It was clear to us from the outset that the New Bodleian's core purpose had now to be reinvented.

Even from the beginning of the competition stage, one could see that the New Bodleian needed to connect more positively to the main group of library buildings. We undertook a simple analysis of the seemingly highly structured but beautifully composed layout of streets and buildings between the New Bodleian and the High Street to the south. We wanted to examine how they related to each other, where entrances and vistas were created and alignments made, and the way that spaces filtered through to one another. Our diagrams demonstrate that there are often

misalignments and that actually the arrangement is not as geometrically formal as one might imagine. One clear axial alignment, however, is the so-called 'Pevsner Walk' which, starting at the Radcliffe Camera, runs northwards through the Old Quad to terminate in the neglected ceremonial entrance to the New Bodleian. While this gives a visual clue that something happens beyond, it is only on the steps of the Clarendon Building that the full impact of the Broad Street elevation of the New Bodleian can be seen.

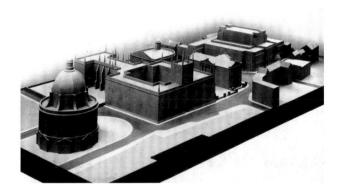

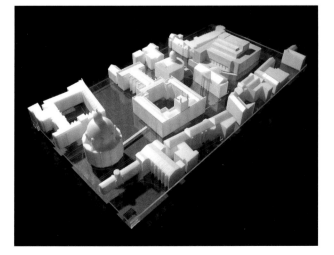

The junction between Broad Street and Parks Road is flanked by the New Bodleian to the north and the Clarendon Building and Sheldonian Theatre to the south. WilkinsonEyre's early analysis of the existing streetscape demonstrated how this could be enlivened by opening up the southern facade of Scott's library.

01 Steps and walls become benches through lack of street furniture
02 Differing paving materials and patterns disadvantage the context of the architecture and lack coherence
03 Road signs, traffic lights and tourist information clutter the space

04 The narrow pavements offer little provision for pedestrians to linger, enjoy the space and look back at the architecture
05 The New Bodleian follows the original street line with an unusable plinth which sterilizes the south-facing part of the site

06 Large open space with bicycle access in multiple directions – which can be problematic for cars and pedestrians

07 University buildings at the eastern end of Broad Street were designed to sit above the rest of the street, which was formerly a ditch. The main entrance of the New Bodleian is tucked around the corner on Parks Road with access via a narrow pavement

By unifying the hard landscaping, making the street a traffic-free zone, removing the plinth outside the New Bodleian and opening up its southern facade, the whole of the eastern end of the street could potentially become public realm, as shown in this visualization.

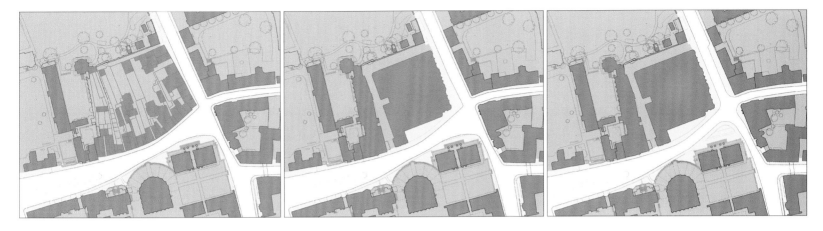

Historic studies show the changing configuration of the buildings and pavement to the eastern end of Broad Street. In around 1935, the New Bodleian site was a complex mosaic of historic buildings, gardens and yards and, with a lack of motorized traffic, pavements hugged the building line. The view south down Parks Road would have been very different, as it would not have been possible to see the Clarendon Building until the junction with Broad Street. By 1946, the New Bodleian had been built; its more orthogonal shape set it back from the original pavement line on Parks Road, and meant that there was a generous area of pavement skirting

the south-east corner of the building as well as a new view of the Clarendon Building. By 2010, changes to the pavement layout meant that there was much less space for pedestrians around this corner, with a more generous 'apron' of space given to the Clarendon Building opposite but less coherent outside space around the New Bodleian itself.

An archive photograph from around 1935, taken from the cupola of the Sheldonian Theatre, shows the terrace of early seventeenth-century buildings on the New Bodleian site.

An image of the library taken in the early 2000s shows the 1968 Indian Institute sitting in front of the south facade of the original bookstack tower at roof level – the massing, proportions and articulation of the extension are at odds with the original building.

The same view, in 2015, shows how the extension has been removed to reveal the upper stack tower, the newly opened colonnade at street level reinforcing the original proportions of the building.

Walking eastwards towards the end of Broad Street along the gentle curve of its southern side, the Clarendon Building is very prominent, and here Scott managed to conceal the considerable bulk of the New Bodleian by setting it back from the medieval building line. This serves the purpose of not only opening up the space in front of the Clarendon Building, but also giving a more open aspect to the Sheldonian Theatre and the Broad beyond when approaching from the west along Holywell Street. Curiously, the very space that Scott opened up is then occupied by the bizarre and unusable plinth, almost as if to assert that the city is not going to claim this anomalous piece of land for any other purpose. Scott's drawings, which are held in the Bodleian's collections, at one point showed a small garden behind a dwarf wall on the boundary line which would have presented a very different character.

Another important consideration in townscape terms was assessing the case for removal of the 1960s Indian Institute extension, which sat at high level on the southern side of the New Bodleian. To paraphrase a famous remark, one could say that this addition was a monstrous carbuncle on the face of a passing acquaintance. Its shortcomings were easily identifiable: the concealment of Scott's trademark vertical slot windows to the bookstacks, especially viewed from the window of the iconic

reading room in Duke Humfrey's Library, and a more subtle veiling effect when viewed from Holywell Street, where it obscured the set-back facade, preventing the otherwise revelatory visual clue that the street was about to open up to form the Broad. In short, it had to go, though there would subsequently be a number of other reasons related to the internal functioning of the library that would justify its removal too.

Looking at a plan of the centre of Oxford it is easy to see that the predominant distinguishing typology is the quadrangle. With the exception of the Old Schools Quadrangle, the others, which are at the heart of the colleges, are largely concealed from public view. There is a strong sense of a secret world of academia beyond their closed gates. Visibility and access is (rightly) severely limited for the public and this enhances the feeling that it is all somewhat out of reach. Oxford's remarkable beauty and history ensure that tourists and other visitors come in droves to the city, so this distinction between public and private has practical benefits too. The New Bodleian reflects this by taking a 'quad' form, although here the centre of the square was filled with eleven floors of books, the outdated and inadequate storage conditions of which were the original *raison d'être* for the project.

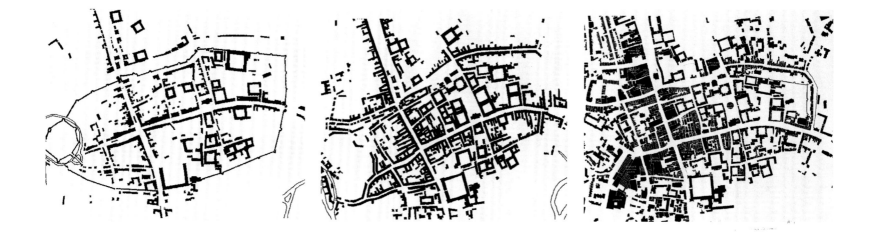

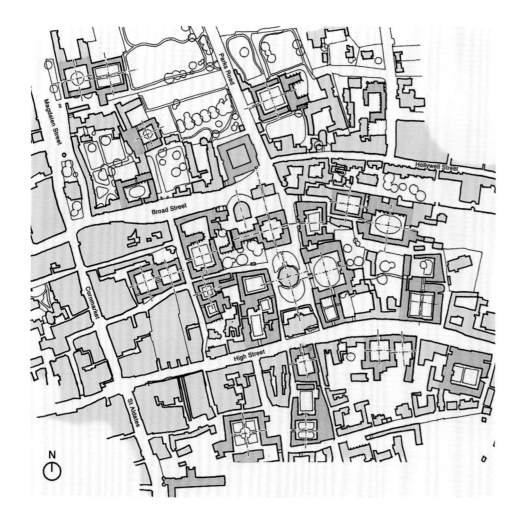

Figure ground plans of the city centre from (left to right) 1566, 1733 and 1999 show that despite the increasing density and growth of the city, the underlying structure of the tightly packed street frontages and the hidden quadrangle has remained remarkably consistent.

The buildings in the Bodleian complex, despite retaining substantial areas of privacy for readers and researchers, each had an associated public space – the Radcliffe Camera presiding over the surrounding square and the older Bodleian buildings clustering around the Old Schools Quadrangle. In contrast, the New Bodleian was a solid and impenetrable block, inaccessible to the public. With the recent remodelling of the building, a ground floor public 'quadrangle' has now been introduced to reflect this 'Oxford condition'.

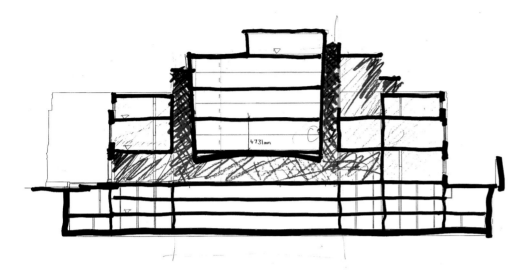

Early competition sketch showing the inversion of volume and void in the New Bodleian 'quadrangle': a key architectural move of the building's refurbishment (top left).

The central stack volume is framed – and given the impression of floating – by the diffuse daylight filtering down through voids to its north and south faces. This was inspired by similar games with light at, for example, Sir John Soane's Museum in London, where daylight is cleverly channelled down into the breakfast room to define the curved edge of its central domed ceiling (bottom left).

Early concept sketch showing a second significant architectural move: the south facade of the building opened up to create a wide colonnade into the public space beneath (above).

Our reworking of the southern elevation is the core architectural proposition that redefines how the building relates to the street and the main library buildings opposite, and in our view makes a significant shift in the relationship between the university and the public. In terms of the internal organization of spaces and functions, almost everything follows from this key move. At competition stage, we saw an opportunity to make the square central area of the building (where the bookstacks would need to be removed) into a covered quadrangle. This would form a grand public space accessed from a new arcaded entrance facing Broad Street. It seemed obvious to us that this would both open the building up to the public, and reconnect and immeasurably strengthen the relationship with the sequence of core library buildings opposite. This space could then provide easy access to special exhibition and auditorium spaces, a shop and even a café. The public would be able to engage with the collections through exhibitions and events, in a sense staking their claim to the national asset that is the collections. To test this idea we needed to be certain that the necessary adaptation would rest well with Scott's architecture and have a positive impact on the setting and feel of the eastern end of the Broad. Exploration through drawings and models soon enabled the vision for this part of the project to be crystallized. The benefits of removing the plinth could easily be seen, resulting in the creation of a usable external space with a southerly aspect.

The south elevation of the New Bodleian as built (top), as surveyed at the beginning of the refurbishment (middle), and reworked by WilkinsonEyre (bottom). Extensive studies were made of the underlying rhythm of Scott's main elevation, with its differing layers of fenestration. From the plinth in each bay there was a broad window stretching between pilasters. Above, substantial punched window openings sit within a uniform wall surface, and then in the next, much shallower layer, each bay is subdivided by pilasters with smaller windows stretching between the verticals. Above this there are punched openings again, but smaller, and above them the vertical strip windows. These strip windows equate to three per bay, but are evenly arranged so that they are read as a continuous sequence rather than divided into a series of bays. This rhythm was obscured by the addition of the extension to the Indian Institute, with its generic 1960s fenestration. By removing the extension, the rhythm has once again been restored, with the opening up of the colonnade at street level serving to reinforce, rather than interrupt, it.

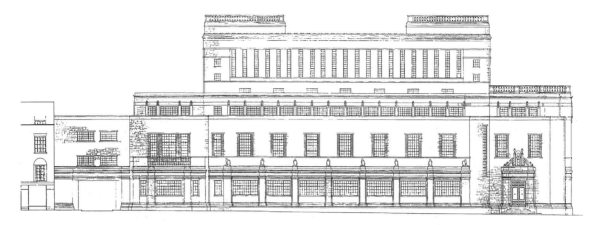

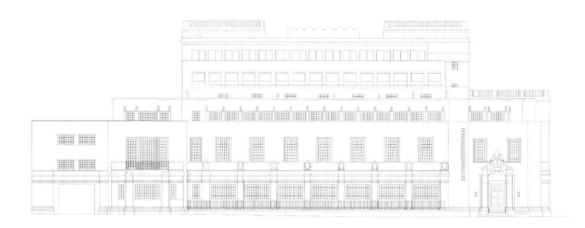

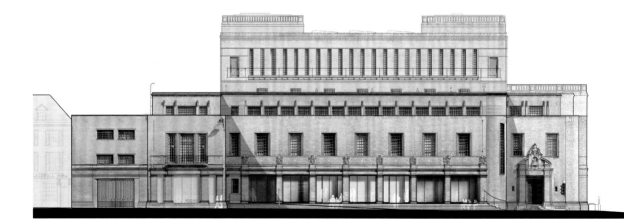

The existing plinth effectively sterilized the space in front of the New Bodleian. An original section drawing dated April 1936 (below right), and a perspective drawing from the same time (top), show that the existing window in the south-west corner of the ground floor was originally proposed as a door, and the existing line of the plinth drawn as a low wall. The door is adjacent to the canteen

room, so Scott's intention may have been to create a private external space for librarians (and possibly scholars) where the plinth was located. A section drawing dated February 1937 (below left) shows this door changed to a window and the walled external space as a solid plinth.

Studies were made of the underlying rhythm of Scott's main elevation, with its interplay of differing layers of fenestration. The upper layer, composed of multiple strip windows, was concealed by the Indian Institute extension, its generic 1960s fenestration breaking the carefully considered rhythm.

The removal of the plinth and the creation of the arcaded entrance are radical changes, but we felt they would make the building feel as if it was sitting more lightly in the street as well as engaging fully with the public domain. I recall seeing Kim Wilkie's 2004 Broad Street plan, prepared for the Broad Street Steering Group, long before I even knew about the New Bodleian project and took a cue from it. Wilkie had illustrated retail uses on the plinth, suggesting the benefits of animating this otherwise off-putting section of street frontage.

The cultural, academic and historic importance of this project made a meticulous approach to consultations with the planning authority, English Heritage, library stakeholders and special interest groups crucial. Richard Ovenden and his team handled the conversation with the constituency of readers, and then we worked alongside him to demonstrate the benefits embodied in the design proposals to the wider group of consultees. We felt very confident in the design and are pleased that it was so well supported by all concerned.

The majority of the accommodation within the existing building was taken up by the bookstacks, which rose up from three levels across the whole of the basement to eleven levels at the centre, and held some 90,000 linear metres of shelving, equating to around six million books. Although far from being up to scratch by modern archival standards, with no fire protection or mechanical temperature and humidity control, the shelving was nevertheless supported by an intriguingly efficient assemblage of relatively lightweight steel sections. The need to upgrade to BS 5454:2000 (and subsequently, 5454:2012) National Archives standards was the most fundamental part of our brief, and the need for wholesale removal of the central core of the building opened up all kinds of architectural possibilities for the interior of the building.

There remained the issue of exactly which collections should be kept in the library, as a book storage upgrade alone would be hard to fund. An extraordinary carousel system carried books in a tunnel below Broad Street to the library's main reading rooms, but this shook the books too much so would never be operationally sustainable. Instead, priceless volumes were carried on foot across the road. There was no opportunity to house appropriate storage or meet the necessary security requirements in the area of the historic core library buildings opposite, so it was logical that the New Bodleian should become home for special collections. This additional aspect of the brief presented an inspiring challenge: what should a research library for special

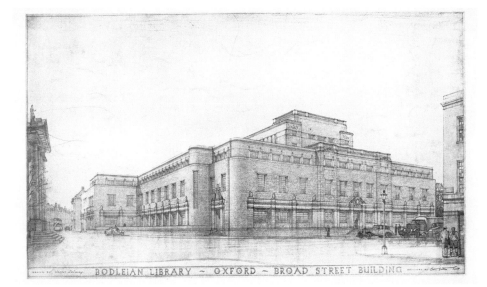

BODLEIAN LIBRARY ~ OXFORD ~ BROAD STREET BUILDING

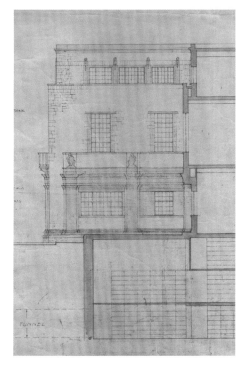

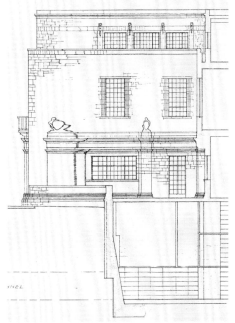

collections look and feel like? And, on a now competitive global stage, how is this influenced by the desires of scholars and the impact of new technologies and methods of learning?

Having worked on the seminal Making the Modern World gallery at London's Science Museum, I am firm believer in the primacy of the original artefact over facsimiles, graphic boards or digital displays, especially when the objects in the collections are so special. These technologies should take a supporting role when the core ambition is to directly encounter the real thing. Consequently the idea of a reading room for special collections conjures up images of hallowed spaces of study, quietness and an atmosphere of calm and intensity. Our initial idea was to create a lofty new reading room on the north side of the building overlooking Trinity College gardens. This was subsequently omitted when the full brief was developed and the financial constraints of the project known. Later, once the quantum of books to be retained on site was reduced, a location was found for a new reading room at high level over the stacks, but within the original volume of the building. This space had all the attributes being sought. Given that we are already up above the height of Carfax, there are unrivalled views out over the rooftops to the dreaming spires. Being at the top of the building, we had the ability to combine natural daylight from above with a tall ceiling height and a clear span, but it is not too large a space to create the desired sense of intimacy. It is furnished with a suite of bespoke new desks, chairs and shelving, all using simple, warm materials.

One of our original ideas for the scheme was to express a 'floating' volume in the central space where the bookstacks would have to be removed. Initially this was itself intended to be a bookstack but it subsequently evolved into a volume housing a variety of uses: the high-level David Reading Room, some reference collections, and the Visiting Scholars' Centre – an innovative new facility for visiting scholars to work and interact in a relaxing, discrete space. This floating volume was to be set in from the perimeter walls to allow light to filter down the narrow gap on either side to the public space below. At competition stage, we indicated a gently radiused convex soffit to this volume, the geometry derived from the distance to the centre of the Radcliffe Camera. Later, the overall built volume of accommodation planned for the floating stack was reduced, which had the benefit of opening up a larger space over the new public Blackwell Hall below. We were anxious to avoid the feel of the type of atrium associated with shopping centres and modern office buildings, so introduced the distinctive linear bands of roof-lights set out on Scott's module. These bring a mellow, diffused light down to the new hall below. This deliberate limiting of the amount of natural daylight not only improves the quality of light but also assists in making the space more flexible for potential exhibition use, where lux levels need to be tightly controlled.

In our initial concept we felt that there was one further aspect missing, and that was the obvious visual evidence that the visitor is specifically entering a library. The resolution was inspired by a visit to New Haven, to Gordon Bunshaft's magical temple to knowledge – Yale's Beinecke Library. Bunshaft placed his bookstacks in a glazed box within a building whose outer rectilinear shell of concrete and translucent stone controls light levels and imbues a sense of awe. Having seen this, we developed the idea of the glazed gallery level, rather like an elevated cloister, which houses the principal open access collection for the reading rooms at first floor level. This meant that one can see not only the books, but also readers browsing or sourcing reference volumes, thereby animating the space. The perimeter of this space is formed by the original enclosing wall to the central bookstack, and we have lined it with a felt-float plaster finish to express its solidity. A series of openings in these walls – each with a differing form – are arranged along the main circulation corridors at first and second floor levels, giving glimpses of activity down to the hall below and animating the corridors.

Early in the commission we made a research trip with Richard Ovenden and the project team to look at particular libraries in the United States, just as Scott did with his clients for the original library. Our first stop was the Harry Ransom library building at Austin, Texas. Here, in a new building, exhibition facilities were included on the ground floor, the reading rooms had ample space between the desks, and up-to-date seminar rooms and book storage were provided. In New York we were inspired by Renzo Piano's Morgan Library with its exquisite reading room and well-equipped conservation laboratories. The New York Public Library included the Cullman Center, a close parallel to the vision for the Visiting Scholars' Centre. We visited Yale's libraries and then went on to the public library at Boston. These visits gave an opportunity to refine the brief and to interrogate their differing operational models, as well as getting to grips with the key differences between public and research libraries. Back in the United Kingdom, the principal team visit was to the British Library, a much larger scale of building with its automated retrieval systems and large reading rooms, exhibition spaces, conservation suite and public cafés. Undoubtedly our thinking was informed by these essential visits, but it also reinforced the approach we took to the scheme: encouraging ease of access; working with the existing architecture rather than against it; focusing on the artefacts (with technology present but subservient to them); and developing a viable operational model for book storage, on and off site, with an uncomplicated retrieval system.

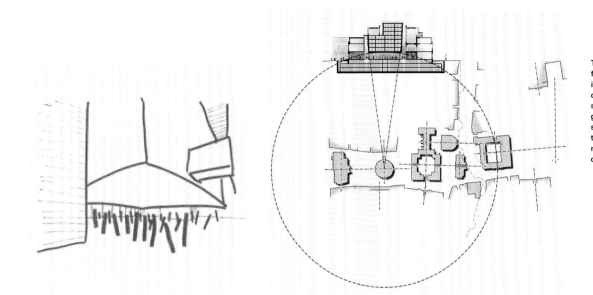

The expression of the bookstack as a floating volume formed the central idea to WilkinsonEyre's design concept from the earliest competition stages. Although later refined, the geometry of this volume was originally set out to reflect a radius taken from the centre of the Radcliffe Camera, the nominal heart of the Bodleian complex.

An early section for the building shows a fluid public space stretching from Broad Street, through the south colonnade and into the area under the soffit of the floating volume. A double-height reading room was also envisaged on the north side. Despite the precise configuration of voids and volume being refined as the design developed, the ground floor public space has remained a focus of the refurbished building.

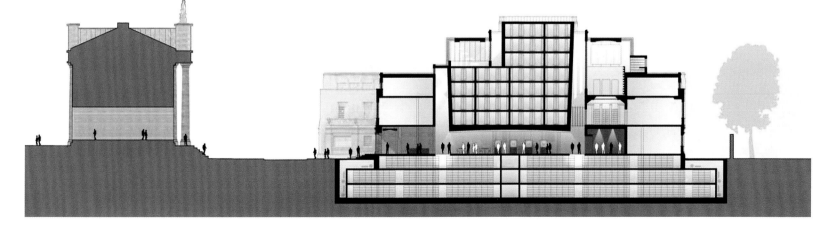

Gordon Bunshaft's Beinecke Rare Book and Manuscript Library at Yale University was completed in 1963. The exterior is made up of five storeys of whitish-grey marble panels which, between the connecting granite frames, are only a couple of centimetres thick. These beautiful, translucent marble panels filter the light to prevent it from damaging the rare books inside.

The glass bookstack which rises through the core of the Beinecke, connecting entrance, mezzanine and basement floors, was an important reference for the Bodleian refurbishment project.

A fundamental part of our approach to design at WilkinsonEyre is that we seek to establish a clear diagram for any building in terms of its major spaces, aligned to ensure the legibility of journeys through. At the New Bodleian, because of the need for public access, we proposed a broad entrance, with the internal square offering clarity to the various functions it gives onto. However, with this quadrangle concept the most important organizing element is the separation of reader circulation and access from secure book retrieval and movement. Essentially the western side of the building, which connects to the bay access road and the new lift and stair core to the floating stack, deals with book movement, and the corresponding core on the eastern side deals with reader access. The existing Parks Road entrance is retained to allow a second route for readers when large events are taking place in the Blackwell Hall.

It is hoped that a plan to resurface and adjust the highway alignments at the intersection with Parks Road and Broad Street can be realized. The intention is that more space be given to pedestrians on the New Bodleian side, that high-quality natural materials are used and that the panoply of road signage, double yellow lines and so on is reduced. It would set a precedent for improving the public realm at ground level elsewhere in Broad Street. The immediate idea is to improve the setting of this most important urban sequence of buildings and to further reinforce the connection between the New Bodleian and its famous neighbours opposite, increasing the physical coherence of the whole Bodleian Library complex.

Inspired by the Beinecke's glass bookstack, colourfully populated, glazed bookshelves wrap around the perimeter of the Blackwell entrance hall. Unlike the Beinecke, however, these shelves are an active part of the library, accessible to readers.

Architectural drawings

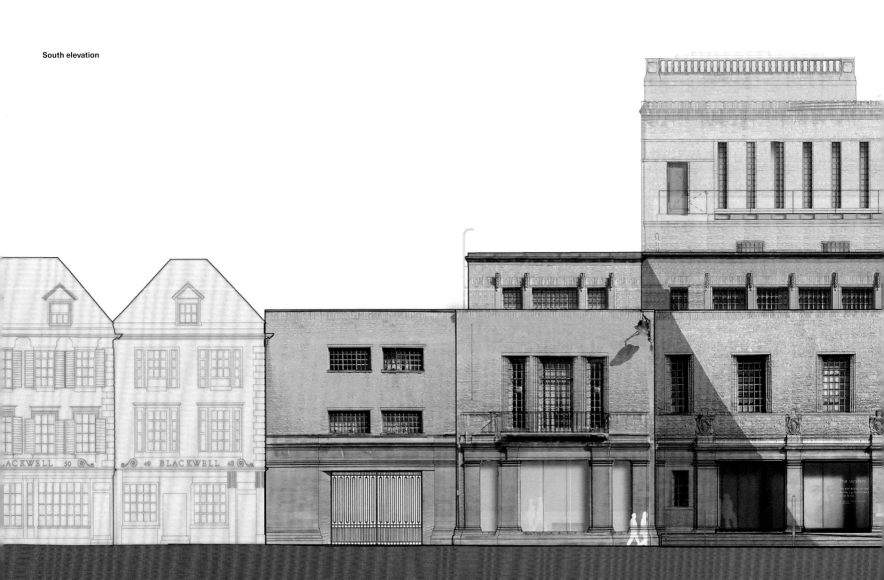

0 1 2 5m

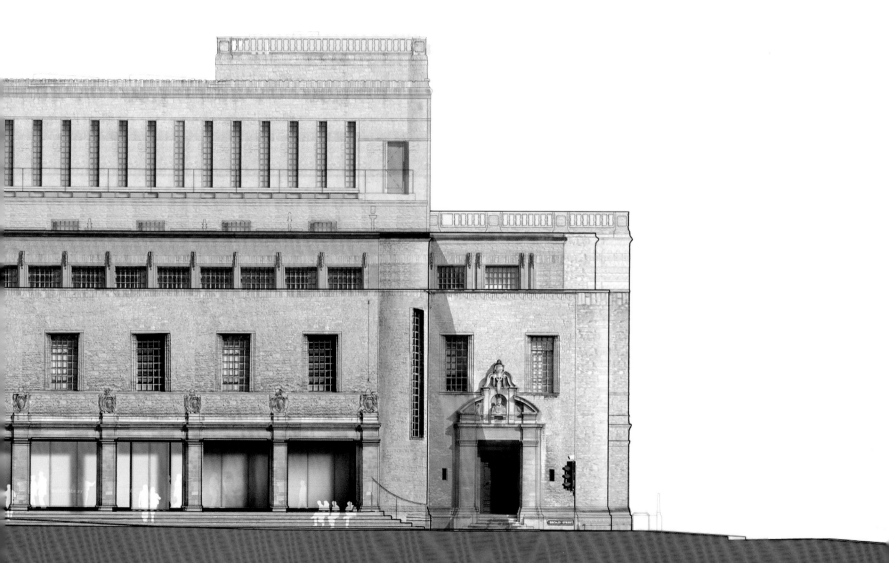

Site plan
Site sectional elevation

1 Radcliffe Camera
2 Old Schools Quadrangle
3 Divinity School
4 Catte Street
5 Broad Street
6 Sheldonian Theatre
7 Clarendon Building
8 Weston Library
9 Parks Road

0 2 4   10m

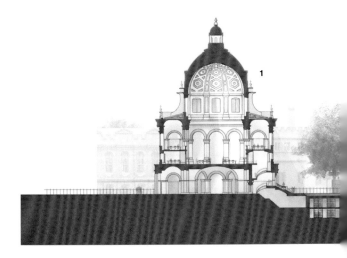

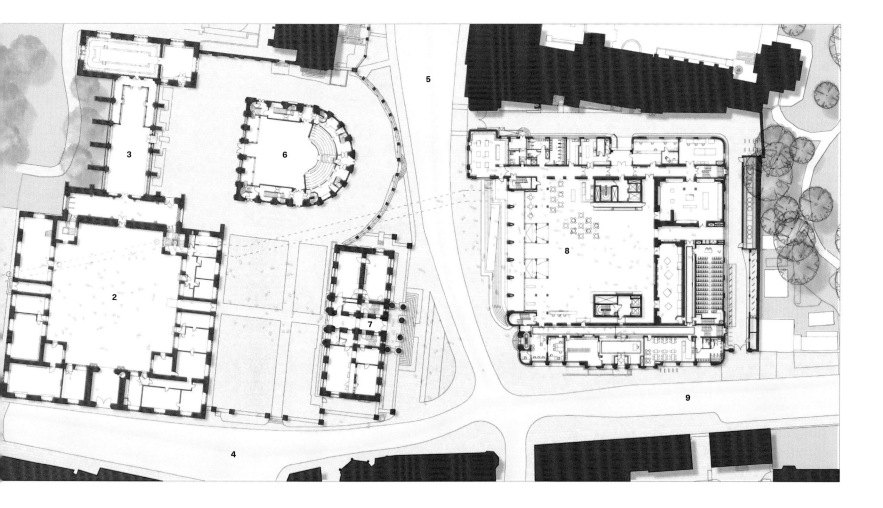

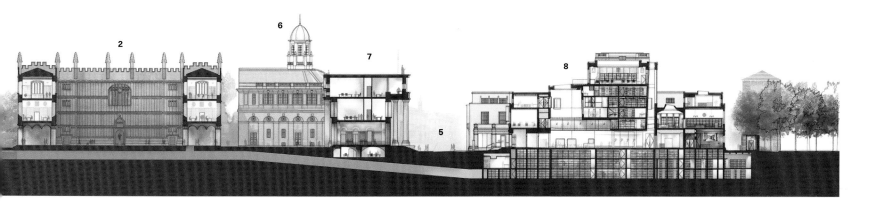

Ground floor plan

1 Colonnade and public entrance
2 Blackwell Hall
3 Shop
4 Café
5 ST Lee Gallery (temporary exhibition)
6 Exhibitions preparation room
7 Treasury (permanent exhibition)
8 Lecture theatre
9 Staff and readers' café
10 Readers' entrance/security

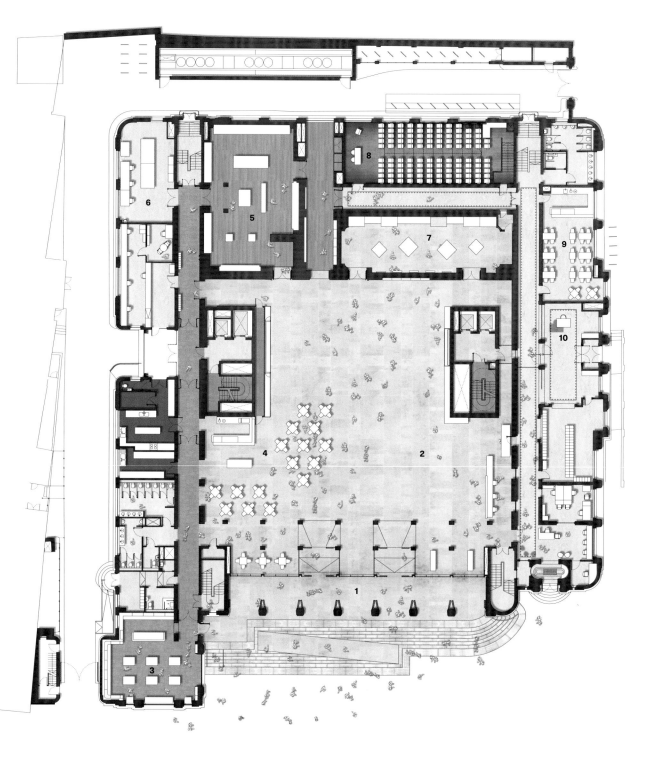

First floor plan

1   Reader enquiries
2   Seminar rooms
3   Breakout space
4   Rare Books and Manuscripts
    Reading Room
5   Mackerras Reading Room
6   Open access books
7   Curatorial offices
8   Centre for Digital Scholarship

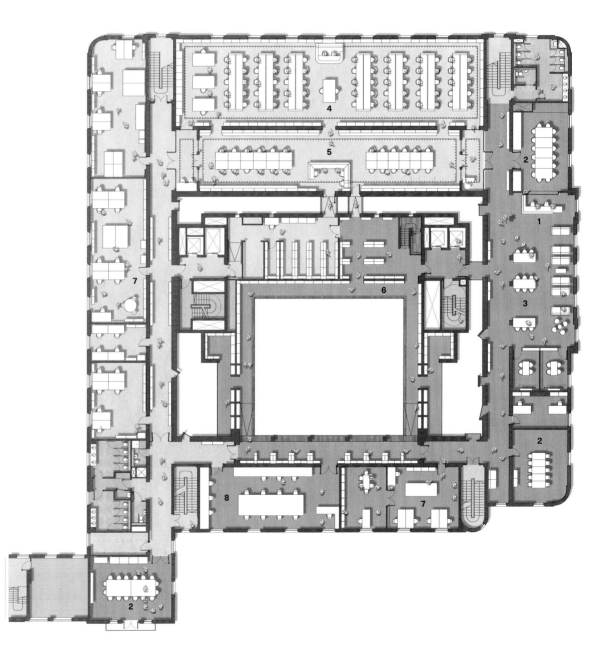

0 1 2   5m

Level E plan

1 Visiting Scholars' Centre
2 Open access books

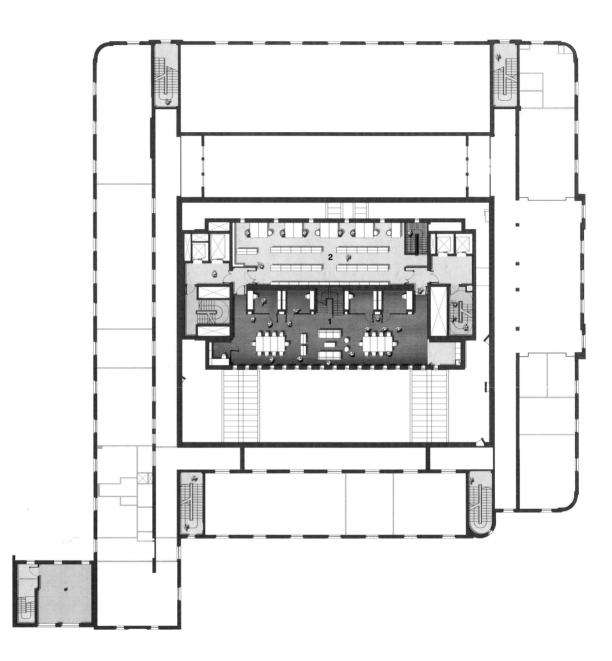

Second floor plan

1 Visiting Scholars' Centre (upper floor study rooms)
2 Secure bookstack
3 Conservation workshop/offices
4 Curatorial offices

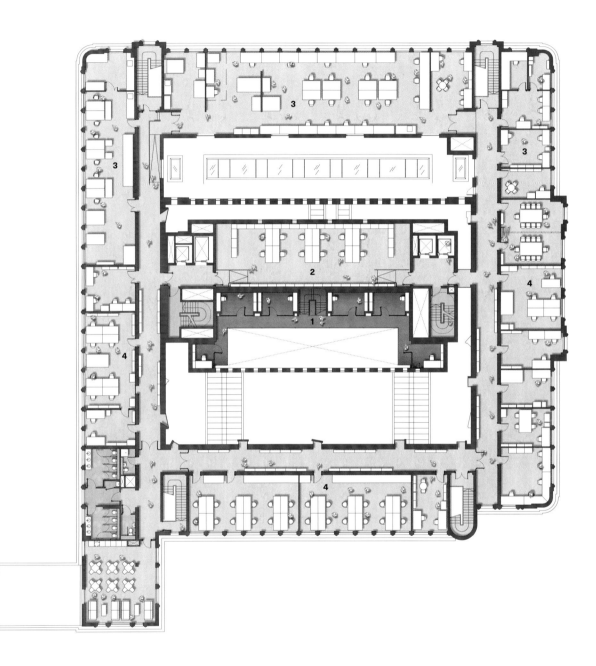

Third floor plan

1 David Reading Room
2 Reserve
3 Roof terrace

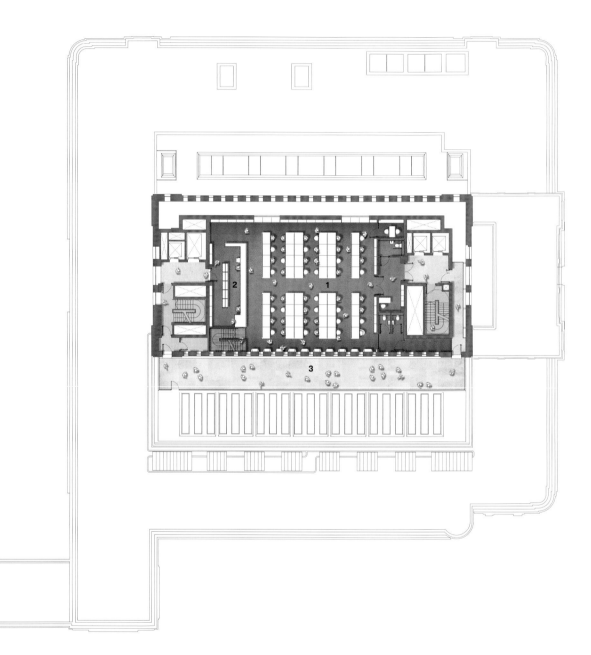

Section T-T

1 Reinstated south stack wall
2 Roof terrace
3 Central 'floating' stack volume
4 Blackwell Hall
5 Curatorial offices
6 Seminar room
7 Staff and readers' café
8 Staff lockers
9 Archive bookstack
10 Plant room

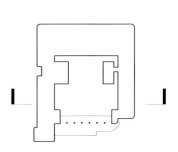

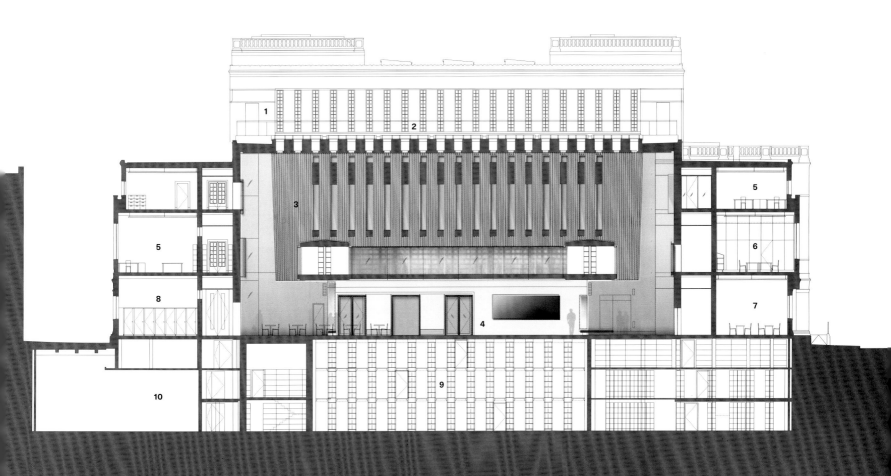

0 1 2   5m

Section R-R

1 North wall of original stack
2 Blackwell Hall and exhibition
   entrances
3 Conservation offices and workshops
4 Curatorial offices
5 Seminar room
6 Exhibitions preparation room
7 Staff and readers' café
8 Archive bookstack

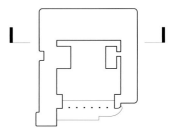

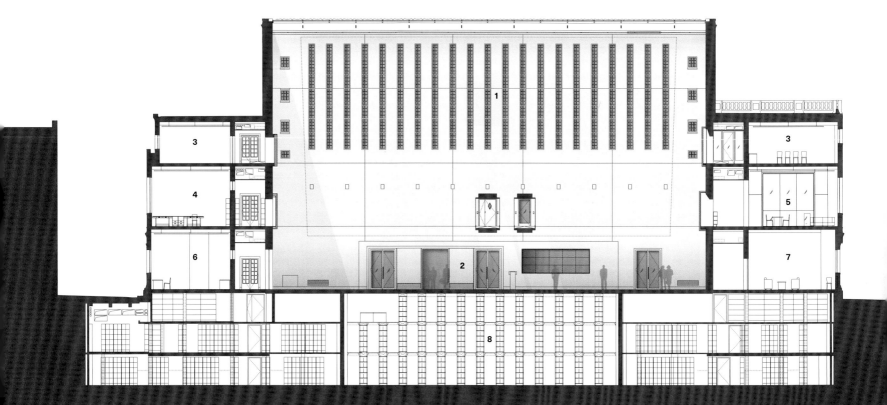

Section Q-Q

1 Plant room
2 Roof terrace
3 East wall of Blackwell Hall
4 Light well above reading room
5 Conservation workshop
6 Rare Books and Manuscripts
Reading Room
7 Mackerras Reading Room
8 Perimeter stair
9 Treasury (permanent exhibition)
10 Stack sorting area
11 Archive bookstack

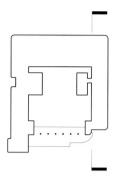

Section G-G

1 David Reading Room
2 Roof terrace
3 Conservation workshop
4 Light well above reading room
5 Mackerras Reading Room
6 Rare Books and Manuscripts
   Reading Room
7 Visiting Scholars' Centre
8 Open access books
9 Conservation and curatorial
   bookstack
10 Curatorial offices
11 Centre for Digital Scholarship
12 Blackwell Hall
13 Open access gallery
14 ST Lee Gallery (temporary exhibition)
15 Colonnade and public entrance
16 Access road
17 Image studio
18 Archive bookstack
19 Existing tunnel

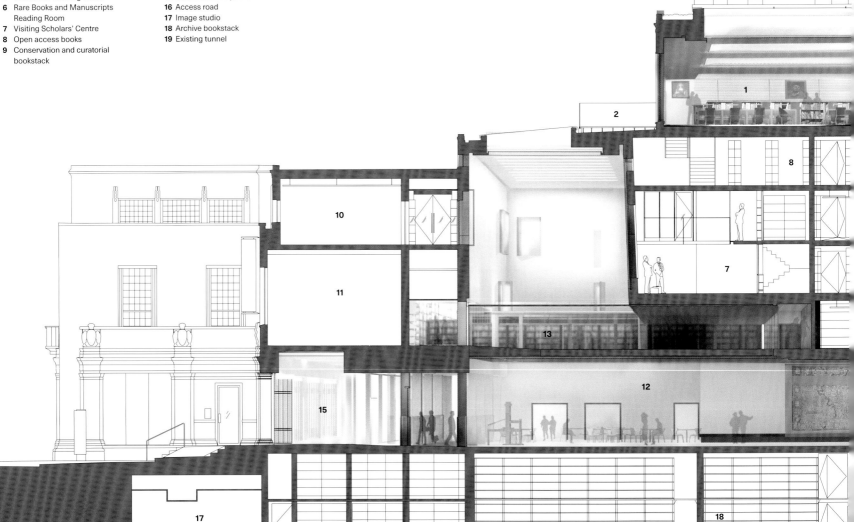

0 1 2   5m

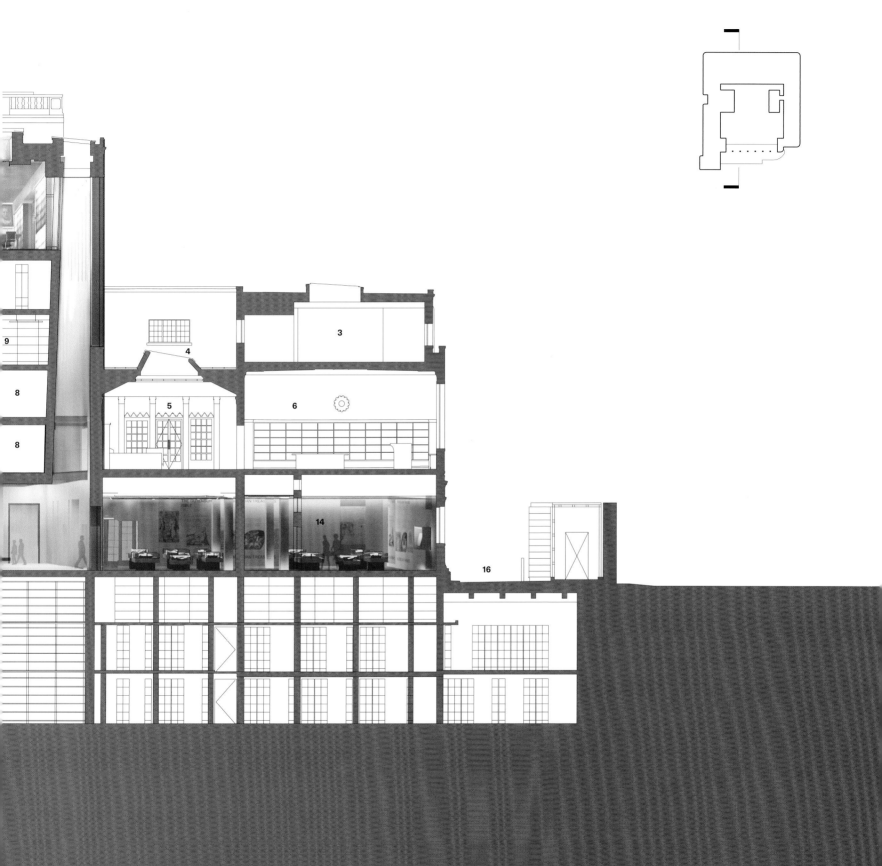

Developing the design
Geoff Turner

Competition and initial scheme

WilkinsonEyre was one of six architectural practices who took part in an architectural design competition for the refurbishment of the New Bodleian Library during the summer of 2006. During question and answer sessions with Richard Ovenden and Toby Kirtley from the Bodleian in the course of the competition, it became evident to us that their aspiration was to transform the library into a centre of serious scholarly excellence while at the same time promoting the collections. It also became clear that the written brief was there to be challenged: the Bodleian was looking to find an architect who could develop a robust and complex brief at the same time as retaining a strong architectural concept and clarity of vision.

In response, our competition-winning design submission outlined a series of architectural ideas, most of which have been retained throughout the project: the removal of the central stack above ground; the addition of two new cores and a 'floating' central stack with a top-lit void at the perimeter; the opening up of the south facade onto Broad Street, connecting with a new ground floor public space and exhibition spaces; and north and south rooftop extensions to create new reading rooms. As we progressed through the early months of the feasibility study, however, it became clear that the primary tenants of the refurbished building would be the books, and their storage, preservation and retrieval would dictate the eventual shape of these design thoughts.

Diagrams from WilkinsonEyre's competition scheme showing (left) the arrangement of accommodation on the ground floor and (right) the basic diagram of the building, with reader access shown in blue via a discrete core, and staff and books entering via a separate core, marked here in orange.

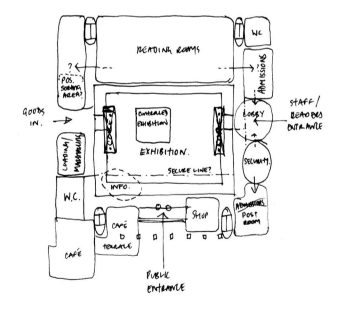

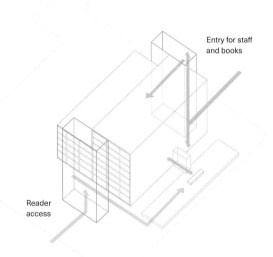

Entry for staff and books

Reader access

A more refined ground-floor plan from the competition scheme shows a variety of activity in the main public space: temporary and permanent exhibitions, café and shop. In this iteration of the design, there is no lecture theatre, and the north wing is a reading room.

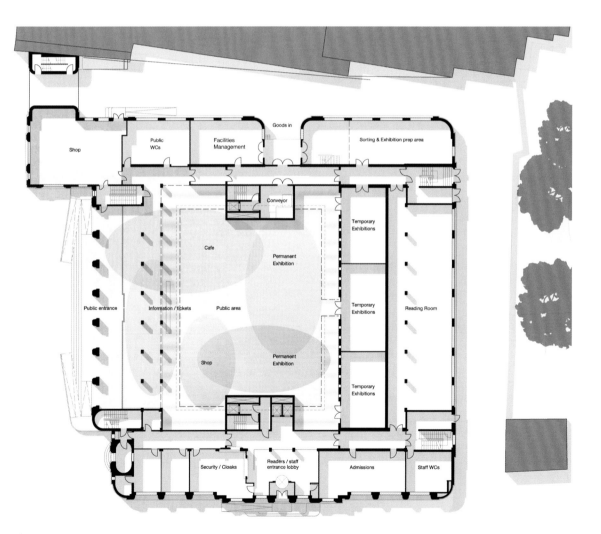

Shop

Public WCs

Facilities Management

Goods in

Sorting & Exhibition prep area

Conveyor

Cafe

Permanent Exhibition

Temporary Exhibitions

Public entrance

Information / tickets

Public area

Temporary Exhibitions

Reading Room

Shop

Permanent Exhibition

Temporary Exhibitions

Security / Cloaks

Readers / staff entrance lobby

Admissions

Staff WCs

Brief development and US study tour

At first, our work centred on operational clarifications and the development of the brief with the users. The accommodation required by each of the departmental user groups – bookstacks, curatorial, conservation and collections care, reader services, reading rooms, public spaces and exhibitions – was analysed and tested within both the overall brief and the footprint of the existing building. We soon gained a deeper understanding of these users' existing and proposed operational strategies, and how adjacencies should be arranged and located. We then analysed the space requirements and related them back to shelving layouts in the bookstacks, storage formats, book servicing strategies and the distribution of accommodation throughout the building.

Not only did we need to address the conflicting and overlapping requirements of archival storage, academic and interdisciplinary research, but we also had to deal with a far broader brief for public engagement and exhibitions. This cocktail of uses was far more akin to the US model of academic research libraries and, during March and April 2007, we accompanied our clients on a study tour to North America to visit a number of institutions which were felt to be relevant to the Bodleian scheme. These included the recently refurbished Harry Ransom Center in Austin, Texas; Renzo Piano's Morgan Library and Museum in New York; the New York Public Library; the highly original Beinecke Library at Yale; and the Music Library of the Sterling Library, also at Yale. Several of them were built to a programme that included public use, and so these visits proved incredibly valuable to our understanding of the project. They informed the design ideas that were subsequently developed, although we were increasingly aware that we would be trying to deliver these within an existing building with very specific constraints.

Following in Scott's footsteps: snapshots from the US study tour taken by the Bodleian and design teams in 2007.

First row (left to right): the team on tour; two views of Rem Koolhaas' Seattle Central Library; Gordon Bunshaft's Beinecke Library at Yale University; Schmidt Hammer Lassen's extension to the Royal Danish Library in Copenhagen.

Second row: Royal Danish Library; roller racking and reading room at James Gamble Rogers' Sterling Memorial Library, Yale; Royal Danish Library.

Third row: the team; external view of Beinecke Library, reading room and cloister at the Irving S. Gilmore Music Library, Yale; library café at Yale.

Fourth row: Renzo Piano's entrance to the Morgan Library, New York; Sterling Memorial Library, Yale; the Beinecke, Yale; the Harry Ransom Center at the University of Texas.

Structure of the bookstack

Images taken during the construction of the library show the density and scale of the original steel bookstack structure.

An initial issue to address was how to deal with the structural design of the bookstack, and how to introduce the floating central volume that was the focus of our original design. The existing eleven-storey central bookstack was a very dense three-dimensional grid of steel columns and beams, and thin concrete slabs. Scott himself had made several study trips to North America, both for the New Bodleian project and the Cambridge University Library, and there is no doubt that the density of the stack, and its integrated structure and shelving, was influenced by several built in the US around the same time. What was very clever in Scott's original design for maximizing book storage, however, was not so good for fire protection. There was no fire protection to any of the existing concrete floors or open steel columns, no means of preventing a fire from spreading and, critically, no effective means of suppressing a fire. Effectively, the existing stack was one very large single compartment, which presented a major risk of fire spread.

We began by considering a number of strategies – including concrete, steel and composite systems – for the structural design of the central floating stack, primarily to assess the flatness and thickness of floor slabs required for mobile shelving, and to see whether it was possible to have removable mezzanine floors inside this central volume for future flexibility. In fact, one of the earlier structural schemes proposed the use of shipbuilding techniques to create a twin steel plate wall, ensuring the tight tolerances required for mobile shelving. Eventually it was decided that the central stack should offer more flexible research facilities (rather than archive-standard stack space only), so mobile shelving was no longer required here, allowing the whole of the floating stack to be constructed of concrete with a steel frame perched on top.

The three two-storey perimeter floors of the building aligned with every other of the original eleven storeys of the central stack, the floor-to-floor heights of which alternated between 8 feet (2,438 millimetres) and 7 feet 6 inches (2,286 millimetres). We explored numerous combinations of floor levels and heights in our designs for the central stack, the intention being to ensure five levels of Nicholson size 'D' books per shelf (i.e. 2,100 millimetre shelf bays) with the necessary structural and services zones. To maximize headroom, the internal floor levels were eventually lowered at first floor level and increased at the third floor, and then spread out between with mini-ramps coordinating with the perimeter floors around the edges.

We also looked at removing the secondary structure and strengthening the primary structure in the basement under the perimeter accommodation in order to increase the quantum of shelving, as well as the possibility of rebuilding just two floor levels of central basement to improve headroom and future flexibility. Both of these scenarios were rejected due to the negative implications of a significant loss of book quantum or headroom.

During this stage it became obvious that the full aspirations of the client's brief would not match the proposed budget. In order to achieve a feasible scheme, the quantum of book storage contained within the competition brief would need to be trimmed down and relocated elsewhere – ideally in the new depository at

Swindon. It also implied that some of the new-build elements in the competition scheme, such as the central bookstack storage area, should be reduced, and it was agreed not to proceed with the proposed rooftop extensions. By this point the majority of layouts and adjacencies had also been agreed, and the structural and services schemes had reached a level where there was an agreed approach as to how to integrate the new-build elements with the existing structural and original heritage fabric.

With the safeguarding of the collections the primary objective of the project, the design of the bookstacks was fundamental to its success. Due to the unique, severe constraints in the existing bookstack, and the technical complexity of bringing these up to

BS 5454 standard while still achieving an appropriate quantum of books, more time and effort went into the hidden underground storage spaces during this period than any other area.

Detailed surveys were carried out in the basement where access was possible, and these were forensically analysed both in plan and section together with the many original Scott drawings and those by Burnard Green of the structural system. Each of the thousands of steel column profiles were also analysed. This process identified over thirty different section sizes which, depending on orientation, could be divided into hundreds of spatial variants within the 4 foot 6 inch structural grid. We developed a series of eight optimum profiles for encasing the

A sectional model (facing west) shows the reconfiguration of the bookstack, with most of the storage now located in the basement and the new 'floating' stack volume above the central public space.

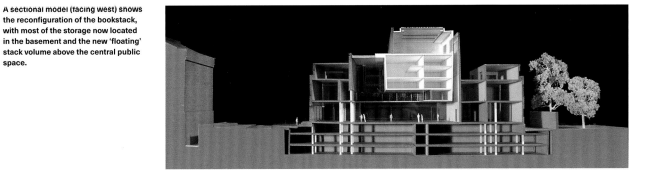

In contrast, a 1937 section of the original building (facing south) shows the extent of the eleven-storey bookstack, and the conveyor shaft (to the right of the stack) for the delivery of books throughout the building.

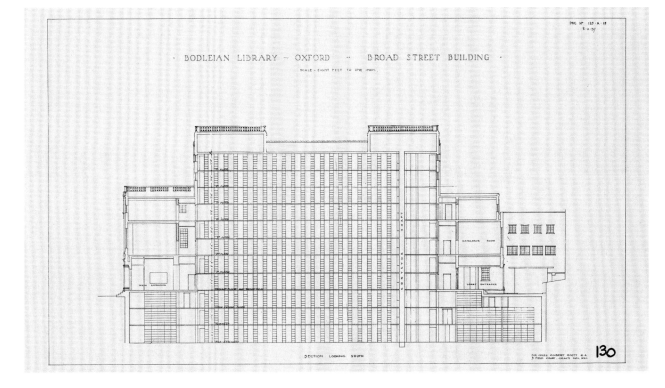

columns in concrete to achieve four-hour fire resistance. This optimization study was carried out in such detail because even 20–30 millimetres of unnecessary concrete cover on each column could mean the loss of several hundreds (or even thousands) of linear metres of book storage across the whole of the basement. As a result, we created a concrete box between ground floor and basement, fire resistant for up to four hours, which was split into seven smaller four-hour boxes, depending upon their proximity to stairs and services cores.

When we started the project we were unaware of the fact that, to keep the structure lean, Scott, Burnard Green and Roneo had designed the stack structure with an upstand beam under the bottom shelf in most stack areas (this was another of the reasons why the original structure was such a fire risk). Within the retained areas of perimeter basement floors we had to address this issue, along with changes in the thickness of the floor according to location, and structural performance. Each area was carefully scrutinized to understand where it was possible to locate fixed or mobile shelving, and where the best place for the principal high-level duct routes within such low headroom spaces should be located. This detailed understanding of the constraints also meant that we could test various options for the shelving layouts to identify the optimum book quantum, and cost per book,

Setting-out details (in plan) for a typical bank of mobile shelving in the basement, and specifically the integration of services (air supply and return, lighting, ducts and sprinklers) with the shelving.

Details of basement bookstacks, here in section and elevation, showing the slim section of the separating floor plates.

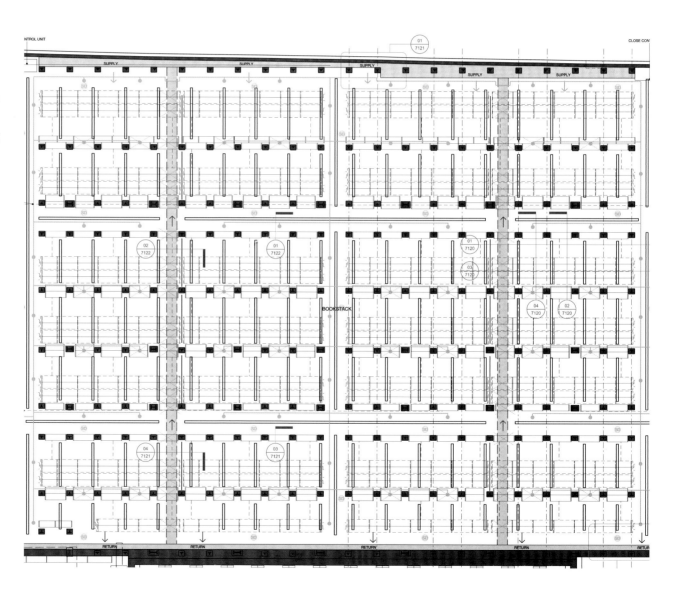

per compartment. These detailed strategies were developed whilst in consultation with the Head of Archive Inspection Services from The National Archives, the regulatory body for BS 5454.

Climate control was another important concern to be addressed in consultation with The National Archives. The New Bodleian was not designed with the infrastructure necessary for modern, archival-standard climate control. In the 1980s three of the eleven floors were retrofitted with a climate control system, but this proved unable to provide stable, moderate conditions and suffered frequent breakdowns. As a result, the condition of some of the more vulnerable library material was deteriorating. The servicing strategy for the bookstack was developed by hurleypalmerflatt, and is discussed elsewhere in this chapter (see page 120).

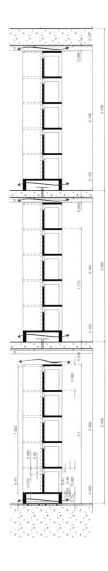
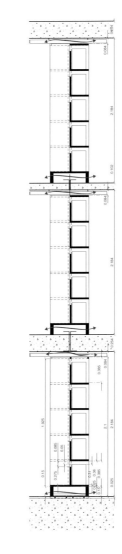
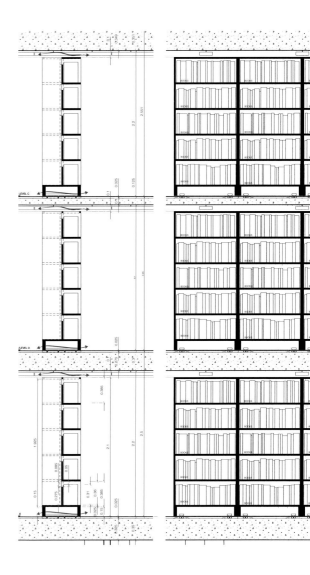

Location and reworking of accommodation

The determination of the bookstack design provided the functional and financial confidence necessary for us to start allocating space within the building to each user group. Although Scott's building included some reading rooms and staff offices, its design is very specific to that of a book store: it was never envisaged as a research facility. The allocation of space therefore needed to balance the constraints of the building with the often competing needs of the departmental groups, and we immersed ourselves in analysing their varying requirements, demonstrating the spatial implications of these and developing a series of options for the layout.

The original building had included some conservation facilities, but these did not support modern techniques (and some functions were housed in other Bodleian buildings). The conservation team's working areas have therefore been consolidated into a space on the north side of the building to benefit from the best diffused light. The department's work is a mixture of workshop and desk-based activity, and by understanding the processes they follow we were able to arrange the space to provide the optimum pattern for their workflow.

Following a detailed analysis of their needs, we broke down the workspaces for the various curatorial sections into two spatial types: closed plan offices or variously sized open plan areas. The Oxford estates team usually specify that all offices should be naturally ventilated, but due to the constraints of the existing building fabric, and the fact that much of the library material the curators work on is sensitive to abrupt changes in temperature and humidity, it was not possible to achieve this in the curatorial offices. Comfort cooling was therefore incorporated into these spaces.

The reading rooms were inadequate in terms of the number of readers they accommodated, as well as their security, invigilation and environmental conditions. Although Scott's principal reading rooms were well-sited on the north side of the building, there were a number of others which were less than ideal in terms of their natural light and solar gain, so centralized areas were created for reading, seminars and research.

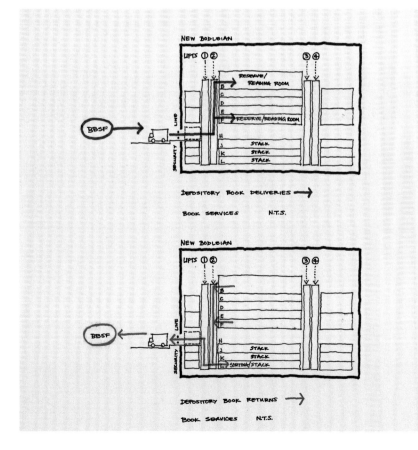

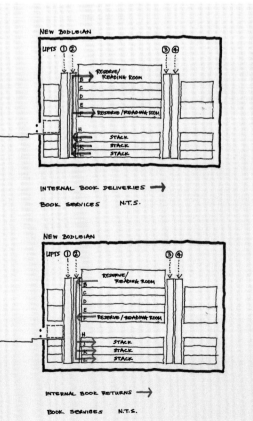

A series of workshops carried out during early 2007 helped the design team to identify in more detail the operational processes of the library, and to understand the relationships between the New Bodleian and other parts of the Bodleian complex. These were sketched out to show internal and external book deliveries and returns, and informed the developing diagram for the refurbished building.

Having mapped these processes in abstract, the diagrams were then applied to the building itself, to explore how the various library functions could be distributed in three dimensions. They were drawn as isometric plans (left), and all related back to the overall section of the building.

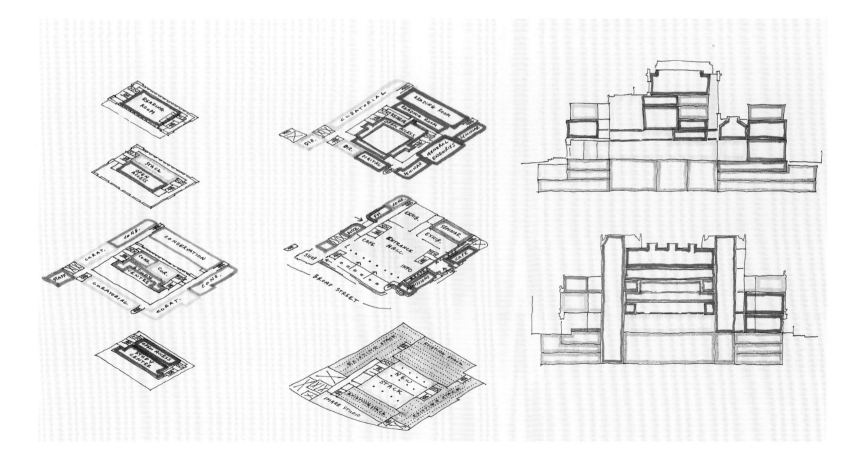

It was essential to test the building layout to see how it could adapt to varying operational scenarios and seasonal demands during this period of the design. Several spatial factors combined to improve the legibility and flexibility of the ground floor. The exhibition suite increased in size to allow for a variety of display layouts, and a route between the two exhibition areas was formed to provide public access to the lecture theatre. Reducing the amount of book-handling procedures carried out at ground floor level created additional space for the kitchen, and by removing the conveyor station the setting of the public café was improved. A separate café for staff and readers was introduced in the north-east corner of the building while the shop is placed in the south-west corner annexe on the building's public facade.

Access zones throughout the building for public, readers and staff were carefully considered to avoid overlaps between public and private realms which could compromise the security of the special collections. Related to this zoning were the arrangements for book handling. Since the completion of Scott's building, the Bodleian's model for book delivery has significantly evolved. To enable parts of the building to be opened up for public use, the stack quantum at the New Bodleian was reduced. High-use modern printed materials were transferred to other library buildings, while low-use materials were removed to the Book Storage Facility (BSF) in Swindon. The Weston Library now only stores special collections material, and provides associated research and exhibition facilities to support this material. Historically, items from the special collections would have been moved to different reading rooms across the central Bodleian site either by conveyor (via the underground tunnel) or by hand, and there was significant risk that the material would be damaged in transit. Reader access is now contained within the Weston itself.

These diagrams summarize the key design moves in WilkinsonEyre's scheme. Starting from the left, the existing building layout shows eleven storeys of above and below-ground bookstack, surrounded by three storeys of perimeter accommodation.

Certain areas of the building require conservation and refurbishment – these include the perimeter accommodation, significant heritage areas (in blue) and the external fabric.

The existing bookstack structure has been removed right down to the basement level.

These moves result in the richer mix of accommodation shown in the diagram (far right), with the bookstack in purple, improved perimeter accommodation in blue, new public areas in yellow, and new upper stack facilities shown in green.

Before

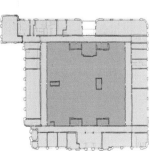

Retained

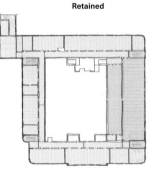

Removed

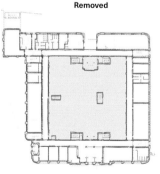

Proposed

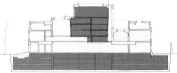

Consultation

During the design development we consulted frequently with representatives from English Heritage, the Conservation Officer from Oxford City Council and the Head of Archive Inspection Services at The National Archives, all of whom had invaluable guidance and input into the design. We also met with landscape architect Kim Wilkie, who produced the Broad Street Plan for the Broad Street Steering Group. We also consulted with stakeholders including The Friends of Broad Street, the Twentieth Century Society, the Oxford Civic Society, the Oxford Preservation Trust, Blackwell's Bookshop, Wadham College and Trinity College. Following such extensive consultation, the planning and listed buildings consent only took eight weeks to be determined.

Sectional elevation of the building produced as part of the planning consultation.

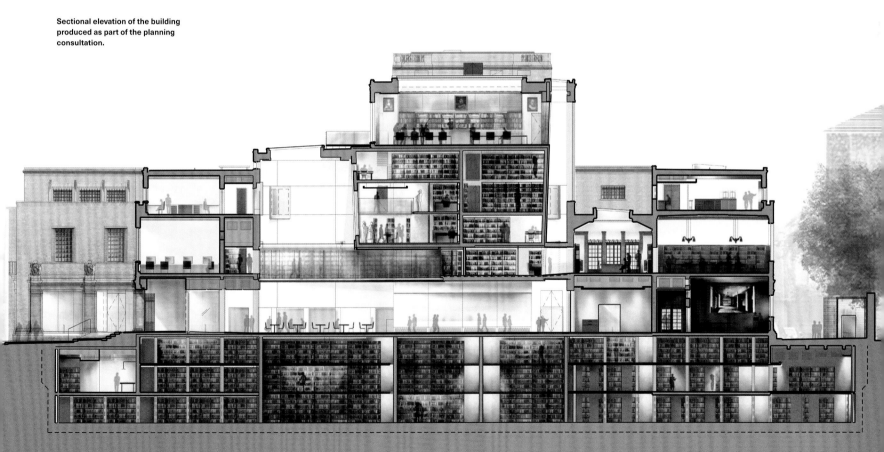

Controlling the environment
Bernard Antieul

Sir Giles Gilbert Scott's original design for the New Bodleian Library was an exemplary demonstration of integrated form and function. The bookstack structure itself formed part of the building's structural frame, with the storey heights limited to between 2.1 and 2.2 metres in most cases. This arrangement was highly efficient for the storage of library materials, especially when sorted by size, and at its conception allowed a suitable heating solution for the spaces.

In the ensuing decades, however, conservation and research techniques evolved, and recommendations for archive storage became consolidated and standardized as the BS 5454:2000 Guide for the Storage and Exhibition of Archival Materials. This was current at the time of the design team's appointment to the Weston Library project (it has since been replaced by the extended 5454:2012 Guide, which also addresses the storage of digital materials), and, among other criteria, prescribed levels of temperature and humidity control and compartmentation for archive storage that were far beyond the considerations of Scott's original scheme.

Creating compliant environmental conditions within the limited headroom of the bookstack required a radical review of the servicing strategy from first principles, drawing on lessons learnt on earlier refurbishments of similar facilities.

Uniform environmental conditions were required throughout the bookstack, but putting the services at high level would reduce the already limited height of each storey, in turn reducing the linear metres of storage available. Increasing the stack storey heights was not an option as it would create problems of alignment with the existing reading room floor heights. High level service distribution was not compatible with the roller racking proposed for some areas of the stack either: an overhead air distribution system above closed roller racking could create air stagnation and the formation of mould on the archive material. The thermal mass of the books in the stack, discussed in more detail below, could be used to reduce energy consumption, but if as a result air conditioning was limited to the main corridors this would result in non-uniform environmental conditions. The smaller compartments into which the new bookstack would be divided for fire control, would therefore provide the basic spatial element to be conditioned.

We therefore developed a concept using close control air-conditioning units – with which the temperature, humidity and air motion can be precisely controlled – to supply air to the compartments through large, low speed supply outlets at one end of the space. This pushes the air towards the bookstacks, while similar, corresponding extracts at the opposite end pull the air across the space, and return it through ducts back to the close control unit.

This concept was modelled with computational fluid dynamics (CFD), a complex computer modelling technique that uses engineering calculations to predict air flows, temperatures and pressures – for example, in the design of Formula One cars to predict downforce and air path patterns before models are built for wind tunnel analysis. Our model confirmed that even though most air passed through the corridor spaces, enough low velocity air percolated through the gaps between archive material and shelves to support the conditions required by the British Standard. To confirm this, we built a mock-up of the longest typical bookstack, and appointed BSRIA (the Building Services Research and Information Association) to measure and validate the CFD analysis.

The nature of the paper, bindings and cover materials of books means that they store energy, so once they have been kept at a stable temperature for a long time, it takes a long time for them to change temperature when moved to a different place at a different temperature. This thermal mass within the bookstack dictated that the temperature of the supply air must be kept reasonably constant and changed very slowly, through return air temperature sensing, over a number of days – rather than over a few minutes, which is the usual strategy. The thermal mass of the books also allowed lower capacity air-cooled water chillers to be selected, as the peak instantaneous load on the building is during relatively short periods when public functions are held in the main exhibition space. At these times, cooling to the bookstacks can be diverted with no discernible degradation in the temperature of the stack.

Ultra-violet, low-energy lighting with presence control was selected to minimize light damage on the special collections in the bookstacks.

A major consideration was the protection of the special collections from fire. We considered a number of innovative solutions, assessing each to ensure minimal damage to the archive material should a fire break out. A high-pressure misting suppression system was selected to actively overcome a fire, but also to limit any negative effects on the collections to mild moisture damage, which the Bodleian's conservation teams are well versed in treating.

The low ceiling heights in these areas required exceptional levels of coordination between the various construction disciplines, and this was achieved with the use of three-dimensional computer aided design tools with clash detection to ensure the systems could be built.

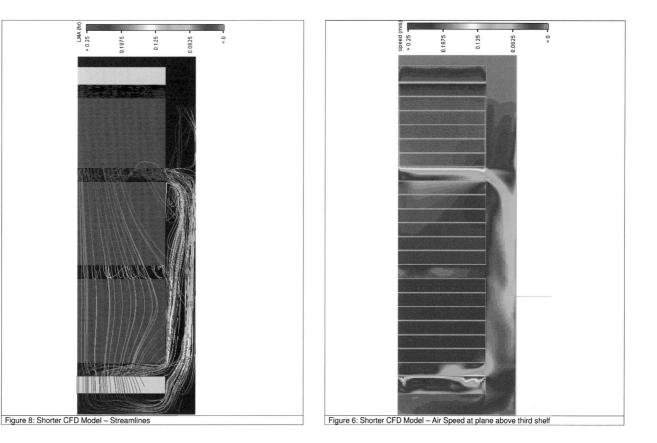

Images from the CFD model, which simulated varying scenarios of air flow and temperature within the bookstacks (shown in plan) to assess whether the appropriate environmental conditions for archive storage could be achieved.

Figure 8: Shorter CFD Model – Streamlines

Figure 6: Shorter CFD Model – Air Speed at plane above third shelf

The exhibition hall at ground floor level is one of the most striking features of the refurbished building, offering flexible space for exhibitions, presentations, conferencing and dining. High-level roof-lights allow daylight to penetrate this deep plan space, but the combination of height and a complex three-dimensional volume presented considerable challenges in terms of the environmental strategy.

The space is environmentally controlled through a combination of underfloor heating and cooling with automatic changeover between the two, supplemented by a displacement ventilation system. This supplies air close to room temperature at low level and uses the natural heat from occupants and equipment to form local plumes that drive hotter air up to the high ceiling where it is extracted. Another CFD model was generated to assist the designers in supplying the correct quantities of air in the right places while respecting the aesthetic and structural limitations of the space.

Specialist lighting with comprehensive scene setting controls was selected to support the multitude of uses anticipated for the exhibition hall space.

The reading rooms and several other areas of the building were specifically noted as areas of interest under the New Bodleian's Grade II listing. Close liaison with English Heritage and the design team allowed sympathetic solutions to be developed to environmentally condition the spaces, with some of the original Scott-designed luminaires recovered and converted to meet current lighting standards.

An exploded plan of the building showing the environmental strategy, floor by floor. The basement, exhibition galleries and upper floor bookstacks are serviced to BS 5454 standard, while the reading rooms, and the vast majority of the perimeter offices and conservation suites have book-sensitive environmental conditions.

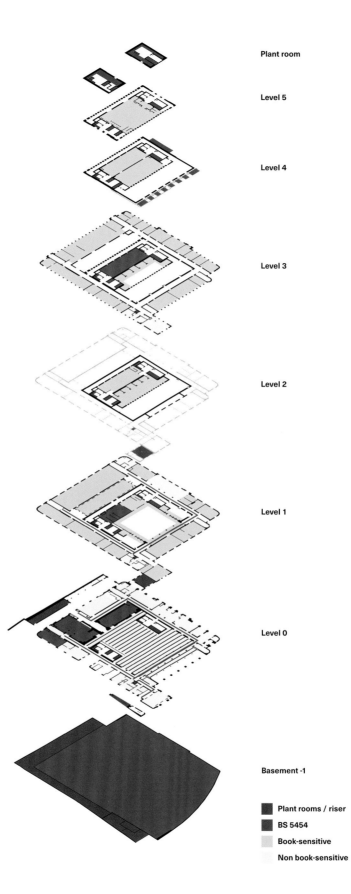

Plant room

Level 5

Level 4

Level 3

Level 2

Level 1

Level 0

Basement -1

■ Plant rooms / riser
■ BS 5454
Book-sensitive
Non book-sensitive

A structural story
Les Chapman

As with many refurbishments of the scale and complexity of the Weston Library, the fact of the building's heritage fabric and Grade II listing imposed numerous restraints – but also offered a number of opportunities for us to exploit as we developed the structural solutions. All the new structural systems we installed needed to live side-by-side with the old ones, relying on their ability to continue performing as desired.

The existing structure, which all sat on a concrete raft, consisted of a lower perimeter block encircling a central, eleven-storey steel-framed structure. Freestanding retaining walls protected the eight metre-deep basement. The structural frame of the central block was built to exactly match the lines of book shelving so that their load would transfer down to the raft in the most efficient way. In between, four-inch-thick floor slabs supported the circulation routes, a pretty revolutionary approach for the time.

The reuse of the existing, 700-millimetre-thick concrete raft was a key element in our structural design strategy. All the new structural elements are founded on it, including the two new reinforced concrete cores (containing lifts and risers for services distribution) which run from the lowest basement level right up to the top of the building. The raft sits on Oxford Clay, and so we had to carefully analyse the possible 'heave' of the raft on this clay as the loading upon it changed. A number of reinforced concrete cross-walls coming down from the two cores were placed below ground to spread the building's weight across as large an area as possible, and a movement monitoring system installed to detect possible heave during demolition and construction.

It was imperative that the library's historic collections of rare books and manuscripts be protected from fire and associated damage from smoke or water. The structural elements surrounding or supporting the bookstacks and exhibition rooms were designed to provide four hours of fire resistance. To achieve this, an extra layer of reinforcement was added to the concrete slabs at the minimum cover that could be sacrificed in the event of a fire.

The challenge was even greater for the existing elements that had to be upgraded: hundreds of steel columns in the basement had to be encased in concrete to improve their fire performance. We used finite element analysis models to assess the columns' behaviour over a 4.5-hour time period of exposure to ever-increasing temperatures, making appropriate allowances for variations in material properties, including thermal conductivity, and the specific heat capacity and density of the concrete.

The new building's main architectural feature – the 'floating stack' above the main entrance hall – is a reinforced concrete box which spans 22 metres between the cores without any intermediate support. Three concrete walls are the main spanning elements. The north and south walls are inclined, and the south wall in particular represents a considerable structural challenge as it is punched by a number of large, uninterrupted vertical slots. The practical solution was to detail the structure as a reinforced concrete Vierendeel truss, named after the Belgian engineer Arthur Vierendeel. He took the view that aesthetics should determine the visual form of a structure rather than the rules of mathematics, and his eponymous structural element consists of a truss where the members are not triangulated but arranged to form a rectangular frame with fixed joints. As this structure was not self-supporting until it had been built right to the top of the box, it had to be propped from the foundation raft right until the last floor was constructed.

New steel elements have been used elsewhere in the building, such as the mezzanine floors which provide the office spaces within the stack. A further, slim-floor steel deck is suspended from the central stack on steel hangers which connect up into the main upper stack walls. This deck supports the glazed ribbon of open-stack shelving that 'flies' around the Blackwell Hall. At roof level, a steel structure sits on top of the concrete stack to form the David Reading Room. This provides a frame for the rebuilt stone walls which, by using stone collected during the demolition works, match the original retained walls elsewhere in the building.

A walk through the building
Geoff Turner

The most striking change to the Weston Library from the outside is the opening up of the colonnade on the south facade, and the creation of a new landscaped setting for the building. Each of Scott's original elevations is classically arranged: the north, west and east facades are symmetrical about the centre, while on the south facade, a formal entrance to the east and a projecting annexe to the south are placed to either side of a central elevation divided into seven bays. In creating the new colonnade, we were very mindful of the fact that we were strengthening this arrangement, and that our adaptations should be true to classical principles of design.

Starting from ground level, where the original plinth (discussed in more detail in Jim Eyre's essay, page 80) was removed, we added stepped access with an integrated, diagonally inclined ramp to give uncluttered access to the colonnade. Like the hard landscape between the Wren and Hawksmoor buildings across the road, we used York sandstone for the entrance, but chose two different types – beige Peakmoor and grey Weststone – to achieve the necessary visual and tactile contrast. To the east, the steps curve into tangent with the existing curved stair tower at the corner of the building, reflecting the way that Scott delineated the original curved steps to entrances around the building – and again echoing the steps of the Sheldonian Theatre across the street.

Once the existing windows, spandrel panels and plinth were removed, the base of the exposed columns was strengthened and we modified the pilasters to form columns. The front faces of

the columns retain the existing Clipsham ashlar stone profile, and on their rear side we added new Clipsham dressings which form a three-dimensional profile to create an oblique view into the colonnade.

Bi-folding security gates, which operate like concertina doors, have been installed to the rear of the columns. We wanted these gates to look as if they had always been there, so their design relates to the proportions of the building itself – they have a strong verticality with a dense base, a more open mid-section and a series of extended verticals to the top. A new glazed entrance screen, which relates to the seven bays of the colonnade, has recessed bronze (or rather burnished brass) perimeter framing to each bay, and two sliding doors to either side of the central axis.

Although the steel frame behind the stone is doing all the hard work structurally, it was a fine balance to achieve columns which are neither too heavy nor too light visually. Understandably, for English Heritage and the City Conservation Officer, this part of the design was critical, and we undertook numerous studies, testing the appearance of the columns in plan and section via sketches, physical models and three-dimensional views, to explore their profile and their relationship to the gates and colonnade.

3D-printed physical model showing development of column profile and gates to the new south colonnade.

View of the south colonnade, opened up to invite the general public into the building for the first time.

Blackwell Hall

Once through the glazed arcade, visitors enter the new ground floor entrance hall – the Blackwell Hall. This is enclosed by three-storey lime-plastered walls to east, west and south, and a five-storey wall with narrow slot windows on the north side. We were concerned that the original masonry substrate of these walls was exposed externally for the first time in their seventy-year history during the demolition phase of the build. So, as demolition progressed floor by floor, a new cavity wall was constructed to protect the stone and plaster finishes on the corridor side of this wall from the cold and damp.

The entrance hall is dominated by the upper bookstack – a 'floating' concrete structure with inclined walls which help to filter light down through the space, and create a tension between new and old. The stack is clad with natural European oak timber slats, which taper and vary in width locally at the corners to address the two-degree incline. The timber cladding also has an acoustic lining behind the slats which, working with the other harder materials, modulates the acoustics within the space.

The soaring, twenty-metre void between upper stack and north wall introduces striated natural light from the original narrow slot windows and new roof-light into the deepest section of the plan. The south roof-lights pick up on Scott's vertical slot windows, but places them in the horizontal plane, in doing so creating a real sense of calm with their filtered light. Even on a bright sunny day, the solar control glass, narrow slots and plasterboard reveals combine to temper the natural light, and create a diagonal barcode of shadows onto the stone floor.

The first floor open access gallery of books has already been mentioned in Jim Eyre's essay (see page 80). To create an unobstructed view of the books on the shelves, we had to ensure the steel structure of the link bridges was sufficiently stiff enough down its central axis so that no intermediate posts or ties were necessary. This enabled us to design an uninterrupted structural glass wall to protect the books. We made the shelving joinery dark and focussed the subdued lighting onto the books to maximize the contrast between their spines.

The entrance hall is environmentally controlled by underfloor heating/cooling combined with perimeter wall ventilation diffusers. Due to the restricted headroom in the basement bookstack below the ground floor, we only had 100 millimetres to accommodate this underfloor heating and the Jura Beige stone floor finishes. We therefore used a screed replacement tile system rather than a traditional sand/cement bed which has a thicker build-up. This system uses a terracotta tile on top of the underfloor heating insulation and pipework. The stone floor is then laid onto the terracotta tile with an adhesive bond. This system has been around for over ten years, but had not previously been used on such a large floor area (here, around 800 m²), so Building Research Establishment (BRE) testing was carried out in 2011 over a smaller area in order to prove compliance with the British Standards recommendations for stone floors and movement joint locations.

A historic archway, which dates from around 1590 and once stood as the garden gate to Ascott Park in Oxfordshire, is now located to the east side of the entrance hall.

Intersecting volumes in the Blackwell Hall: the floating stack; café culture at ground floor level; and animated, open access bookshelves around the perimeter of the void above.

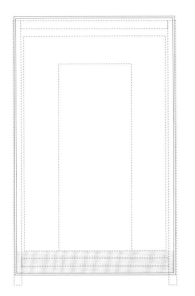

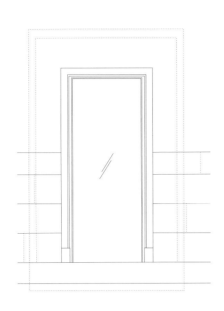

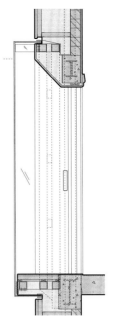

The walls of the main void above the Blackwell Hall are punched with a sequence of openings which correspond with perimeter corridors to the first and second floors. Some are new openings, while others reuse existing openings into the old central bookstack.

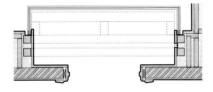

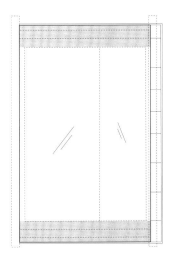
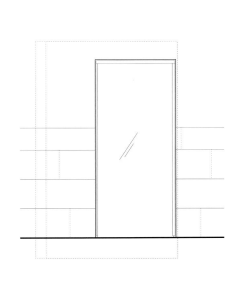
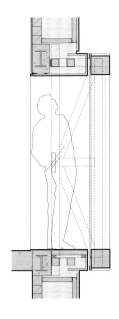

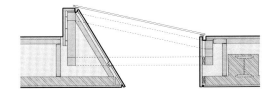

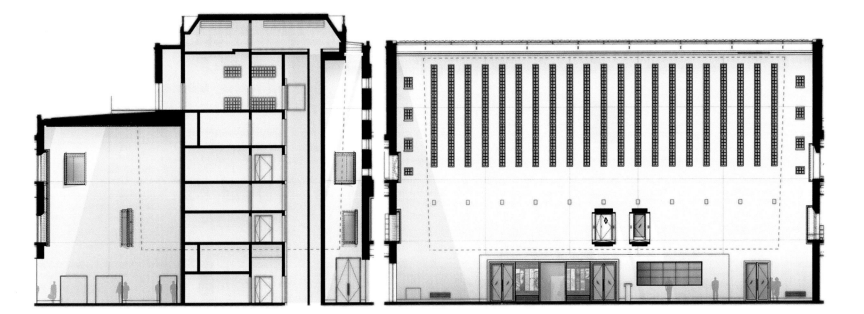

The openings have been designed as contemporary interpretations of an oriel window, and are articulated in a variety of ways: some are simple glazed slots, some project out to frame views into the hall below, while others have an integrated reading seat.

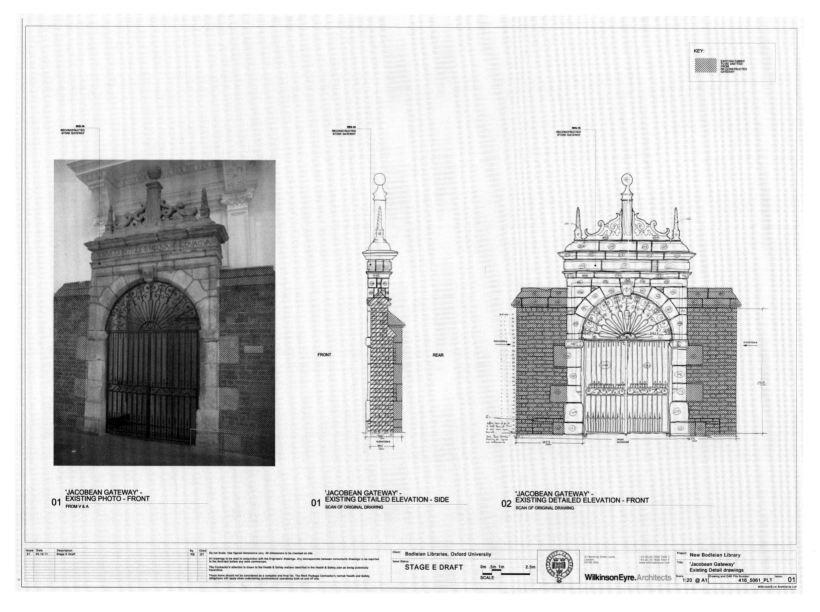

'JACOBEAN GATEWAY' -
01 EXISTING PHOTO - FRONT
FROM V & A

'JACOBEAN GATEWAY' -
01 EXISTING DETAILED ELEVATION - SIDE
SCAN OF ORIGINAL DRAWING

'JACOBEAN GATEWAY' -
02 EXISTING DETAILED ELEVATION - FRONT
SCAN OF ORIGINAL DRAWING

KEY:
EXISTING FABRIC TO BE OMITTED FROM RE-CONSTRUCTED GATEWAY

FRONT   REAR

Client: Bodleian Libraries, Oxford University

Issue Status:
STAGE E DRAFT   0m .5m 1m   2.5m
SCALE

WilkinsonEyre. Architects

Project: New Bodleian Library
Title: 'Jacobean Gateway'
Existing Detail drawings

Scale: 1:20 @ A1   Drawing and CAD File Number: 416_5061_PLT   Issue 01

This sixteenth-century stone gateway from Ascott Park in Stadhampton, Oxfordshire, acts as a portal for scholars and readers to enter the secure east wing of the ground floor from the Blackwell Hall. The entablature of the archway bears the Latin inscription 'SI BONVS ES INTRES: SI NEQVAM NEQVAQVAM', which translates as 'If you are good, enter. If wicked, by no means.'

Little is known of the original Ascott House, the ancestral home of the Dormer family. It was rebuilt in around 1660 but destroyed by fire just two years later in 1662. This garden gateway survived on the estate for over three hundred years but was taken down in 1925 and gifted to the Victoria and Albert Museum. There, it was rebuilt and put on display until the galleries were replanned in the 1990s and the arch was removed to the museum's storage facility. For conservation reasons, it was not

possible to re-erect the gateway at Ascott Park, but the creation of the Weston Library provided an opportunity to return it to public view in its home county as a long-term loan from the museum.

Overleaf:
Visitors in the Weston Library's new
orientation space and internal
'quadrangle' – the Blackwell Hall.

North wing

A new suite of exhibition and lecture theatre rooms in the library's north wing, entered from the Blackwell Hall, has met the Bodleian's desire to improve public access to the library, its treasures and research activity of its users. A portion of the original bookstack has been removed from directly under the Mackerras Reading Room, creating a new double-height ground floor space. To the west, the ST Lee Gallery for temporary exhibitions has been constructed, and to the east, the Bodleian Treasury, both served by an exhibitions preparation area where the curatorial team can develop ideas for display content and layout.

Both exhibition galleries are conditioned for temperature and humidity control to ensure compliance with exhibition standards, in turn allowing the display of rare and fragile items from the Bodleian collections. While the Treasury has been designed (by others) with specific content in mind, the cases in the temporary gallery were developed in close conjunction with the exhibitions team to create a broad range of display possibilities, enabling them to bring the collections to life for the public. The two galleries and preparation area are all individually compartmentalized to ensure fire protection and also the necessary levels of security.

To the north-east corner of the north wing is a new 112-seat lecture theatre, fitted with tiered and flat seating to gain optimum sightlines within the constraints of the existing volume. Each seat has integrated power and a writing tablet, and the audio-visual infrastructure and equipment is fully integrated into the room. Acoustic finishes have been applied to the ceiling bulkheads, walls, floors and furniture. The control desk, lectern and high table are of bespoke joinery to be consistent with other elements within the room and elsewhere in the building.

Also in the north wing, and at second floor level, are the new conservation workshops. Here the north wall of the existing perimeter corridor has been removed to create an airy open-plan workshop. The blocked-up roof-lights in this area have been reinstated and refurbished, and several new ones formed, to give the correct amount of daylight for the highly skilled work of the Conservation and Collections Care Team.

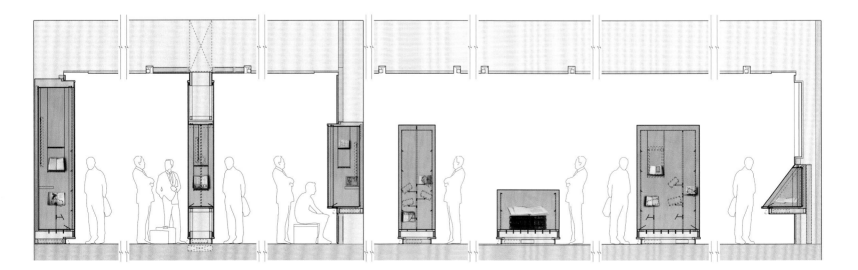

Drawings showing possible
arrangements of the display cases in
the temporary exhibitions gallery, (left)
in section and (right) in plan.

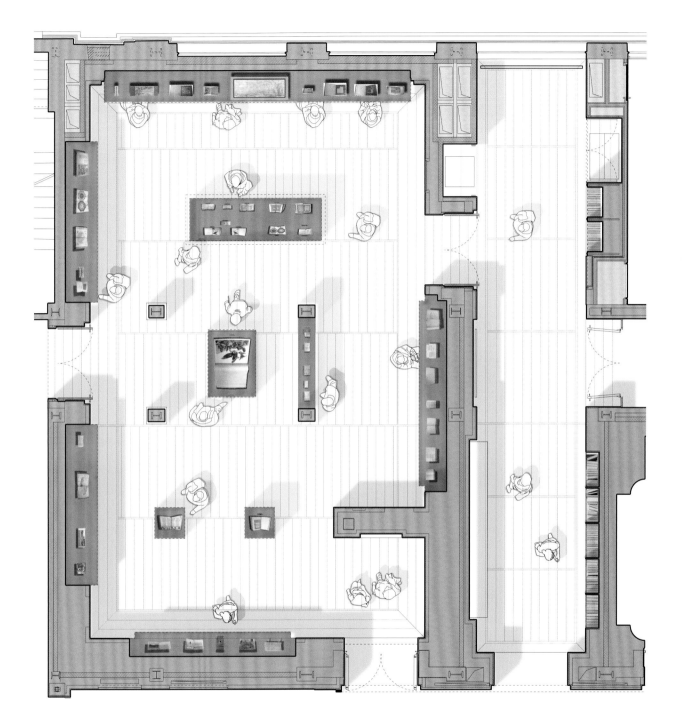

The temporary exhibitions gallery is furnished with flexible cases, allowing a wide range of books, objects and ephemera to be displayed. However, the remit of the Bodleian's exhibition team extends beyond the formal galleries to include other parts of the building – for example the Blackwell Hall, where the sixteenth-century Sheldon Tapestry Map of Worcestershire is on permanent display, following extensive conservation.

In the inaugural exhibition, *Marks of Genius*, a bust of Isaac Newton looks out over other treasures from the collections.

East wing

The east wing of the building – particularly at ground floor level – is one of the most important areas in terms of architectural heritage. An entrance hall from Parks Road links to the east corridor, and in turn to the curved vestibule area in the south-eastern corner of the building where the King George VI door is located. The primary work here was to refurbish and conserve the existing finishes, as well as introducing effective yet understated security lines and improving the natural daylighting throughout.

A Taynton stone veneer was used by Scott throughout for the walls, carved cornices, classical mouldings, friezes, door surrounds and counter, and this has been carefully cleaned and repaired. Where new openings have been introduced into the east corridor wall, these have been given stone reveals and architraves to reflect the style of the Scott originals. Facilities for staff and readers are also located here – to the south of the entrance hall, locker storage, and to the northern end of the corridor, a new café.

An original photograph of the east entrance (opposite left) shows the extent of the Taynton stone veneer and finishes, while an image taken before the refurbishment shows the incremental cluttering of the space (opposite right).

Drawings showing the ground floor east corridor in elevation (above) and plan (below). The south-east entrance can be seen to the left of the plan, and the new readers' café to the right.

Panoramic view of the east facade following cleaning, composed symmetrically around the central readers' entrance.

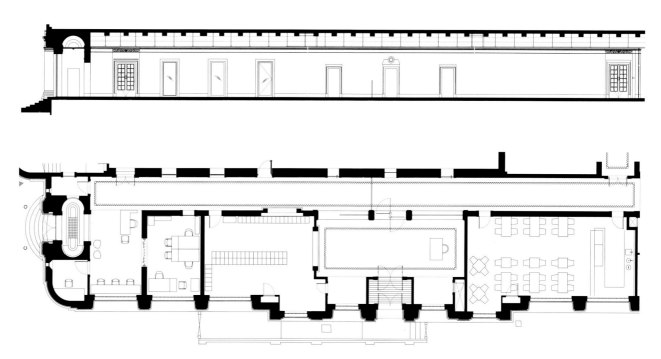

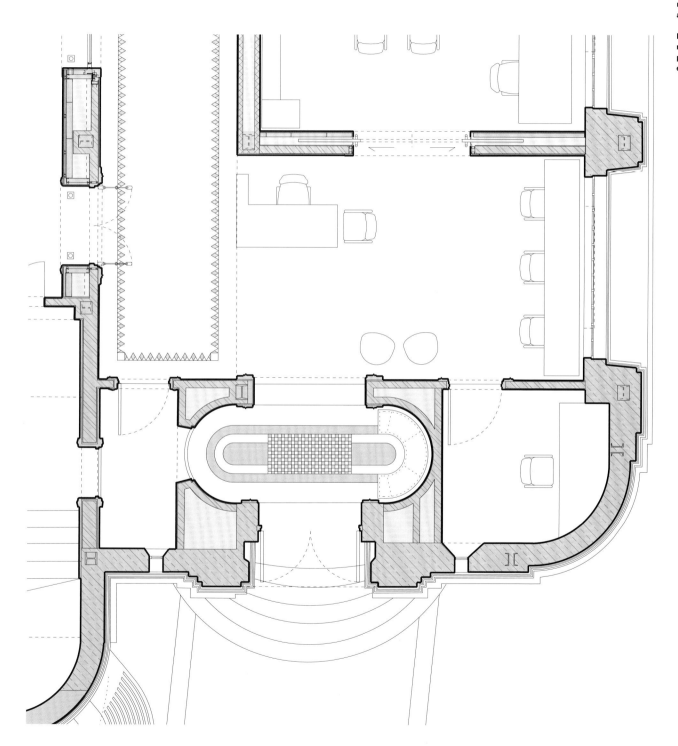

The restored east entrance and corridor area, (left) with glimpses through into the Blackwell Hall (lower left). The vestibule immediately inside the King George VI door has also been refurbished, and a curved bench added in the eastern recess (right).

Drawing showing the layout of the new admissions area off the previously unused south-east entrance to the building.

Visiting Scholars' Centre

The Visiting Scholars' Centre is a research facility at the heart of the library which aims to nurture an interdisciplinary research community, where visiting fellows can work on their own projects, making use of the Bodleian's special collections and contributing to intellectual exchange within the wider university. Here, two levels of cellular offices are arranged around a central double-height communal space. Inclined glazed strip windows, echoing Scott's original windows, provide the space with views down into, and borrowed light from, the south side of the Blackwell Hall.

All of the individual offices are lined in bespoke joinery, with metal and glazed partitions which are divided up by timber shelving. The mezzanine floor (where the upper level of offices is located) is partly suspended from the floor above, to help minimize the floor depth required – and in so doing maximize headroom.

The Visiting Scholars' Centre is tucked into a volume at the very heart of the building. Its central space is flanked to the north by a bank of glass-screened study rooms, and to the south by a wall of vertical slot windows which look down into the Blackwell Hall below. The central space offers an informal environment for visiting scholars to interact and share the findings of their research.

The centre currently offers eighteen fellowships that run for between one and nine months. Individual study rooms provide a home-from-home for the visiting fellows.

The Mackerras Reading Room

This room is one of two Scott-designed rooms located on the north side of the building at first floor level, and was previously the PPE Catalogue Room.

The original readers' entrance sequence into the east end of this room, via the bronzed metal and glass screens and doors off the general enquiries space, has now been reinstated, and acoustic glazed screens and doors inserted to form a new security lobby and consultation room at either end.

From Scott's drawings we were able to ascertain that he originally intended to locate a reserve desk in the centre of the room adjacent to the central bookstack, but this was never actually built. However, it seemed natural to position the new reserve desk in the same location, benefitting from its relationship to the new central reserve area.

The original roof-lights were blocked up during World War II and never reopened. As part of the refurbishment works they have been opened up once more, and a new roof-light installed with bulkheads which follow the profile of the chamfered ceiling inside the room. The triple glazing was specified to respond to the needs of both readers and books, the glass providing even and natural diffused daylight into the room, and preventing ultra-violet and direct sunlight from harming the books. The original metal framing to the lower section of roof-light has been reinstated and refurbished, and helps to provide a linear order to the room.

Two new openings have been formed between the Mackerras Reading Room and the Rare Books and Manuscript Reading Room, enabling these two rooms to be served by a single reserve desk.

One of the most challenging aspects of design coordination in this room, and indeed across the whole project, was the integration of the heating and ventilation systems into the fabric of the building so that the original architecture was displayed to its full effect. Air-conditioning units located in the lobby ceilings at either end of the room supply horizontal ducts which run in the triangular void of the chamfered ceiling. The cooled air then passes through vertical ducts hidden in the south wall and feeds into the room through grilles in the skirtings of the shelf units. Stale air is removed through a slot which runs around the perimeter of the chamfered part of the ceiling.

The east–west longitudinal perspective of the room has been strengthened by the bespoke design of the perimeter shelving and readers' tables, and the reinstated perimeter flooring pattern. The shelving has been designed with a chamfered reading surface, and the Taynton square columns, carved cornice and perimeter frieze and ornate bronze screens have all been refurbished.

The new Mackerras Reading Room is located in the former PPE Catalogue Room, which originally had shelves to either side and a clear floor space in the centre. By the early 2000s, the room's roof-lights were blocked from the exterior. The original linoleum floor was replaced with carpet, freestanding bookshelves installed in front of the bronze screens, and fluorescent light used to illuminate the room.

Plans and elevations showing the space reconfigured as a reading room.

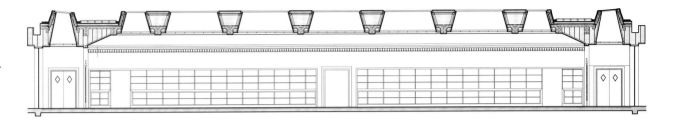

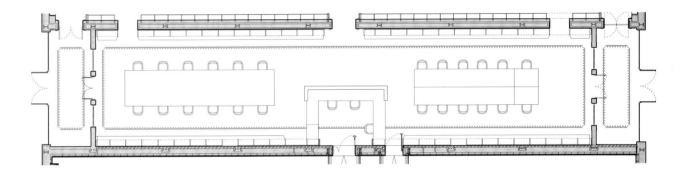

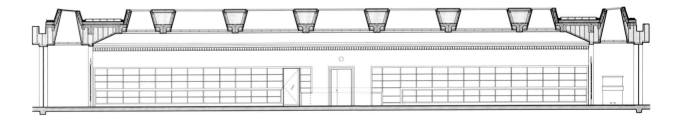

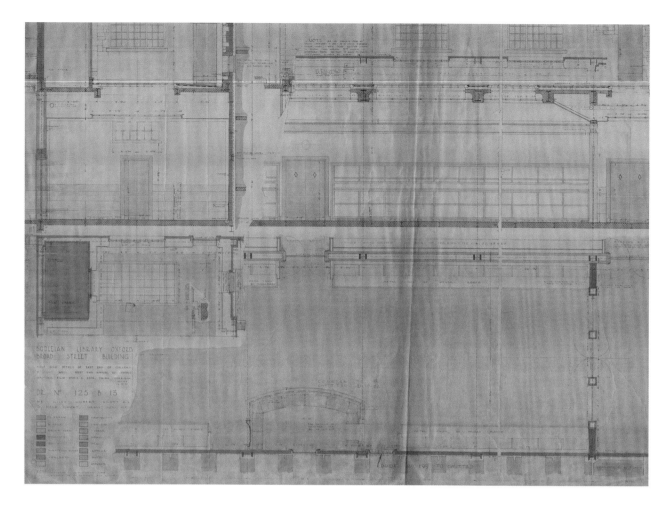

Original Scott drawing of the PPE Catalogue Room, with the roof-lights clearly shown in the longitudinal section to the top right of the drawing.

Sectional drawing showing the reinstated roof-lights.

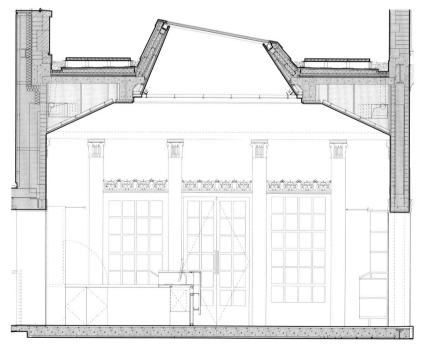

With its roof-lights, flooring, metalwork and joinery restored and renewed, and open access shelving added to either side, the Mackerras Reading Room is now a naturally lit space for focused study once more.

Rare Books and Manuscript Reading Room

This room, formerly the PPE Reading Room, has a number of original features which were specifically designed for the space. All of them – the inlaid wood ceiling, stylized wood chandeliers, large north-facing aluminium windows, perimeter sapele mahogany book shelves, timber clock, enquiries desk, and readers' tables and chairs – have been refurbished and, where necessary, modified.

Again, an important concern was how to integrate new services into the heritage fabric and furniture to meet modern library standards of access, environment and security in an architecturally sensitive way. The most prominent visual changes are the amendments to the desk and readers' tables, which have significantly improved the operational and security functionality of the room.

The former issue desk has been carefully modified and refurbished, and relocated to a central position within the room to act as an invigilation desk. The corners of the desk – one of which is original and one newly crafted – display beautiful joinery, with a concave double curve in a fiddle-back veneer pattern. The original Scott-designed readers' tables have been modified to simplify sight lines across the room, and to increase the available space per reader. This has been achieved by removing the vertical hood and replacing it with slim-profile task lights, increasing the depth of the table top by 200 millimetres per reader, and adding a central band of gilding metal which incorporates a flap for power.

Similarly the Scott-designed bucket chairs and easy back chairs have been refurbished and reupholstered with matching leather to that of the new Bodleian chair.

The original wooden chandeliers have been refurbished and new bespoke ones made to match for the opposite end of the room. These were made by specialist heritage lighting subcontractors, who have worked on a number of original fittings throughout the building. Around the perimeter of the room uplighters are concealed on top of shelves to wash the walls and timber ceiling with light. Downlighting has also been provided to illuminate the book spines on the shelves. The heating and cooling ventilation strategy is similar to Scott's original: along the north wall, fan coil units have been integrated into existing niches beneath each window and between the shelves.

Outside these two main reading rooms are the general enquiries area and seminar rooms. The enquiries area has been created by removing five sections of the east corridor's partition wall. With its high soffit and large windows, this open-plan area has a relaxed, informal feel compared to the quiet focus of the reading rooms. Two new seminar rooms are located at either end of the corridor, offering space for visiting groups of students and researchers to view and discuss aspects of the library's work, while two smaller meeting rooms open directly off the central general enquiries space.

Much of the original joinery of the PPE Reading Room (formerly known as the Commonwealth Room), including the inlaid wood ceiling, chandeliers, shelves and desks, remained intact. As found, the room retained its original purpose as the main reading room within the New Bodleian, arranged with bookshelves around the perimeter and long reading desks in the centre of the room, and the issue desk positioned to the east.

Plans and elevations showing the space retained as a reading room for special collections.

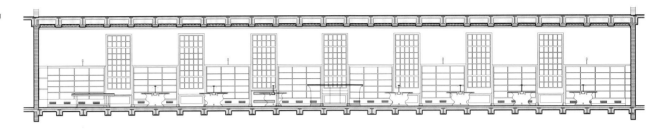

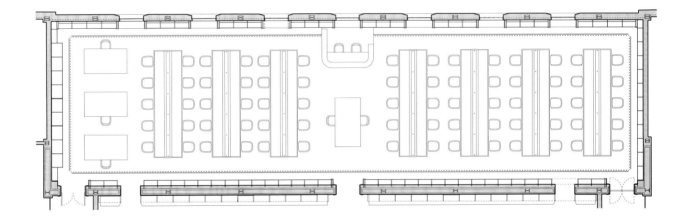

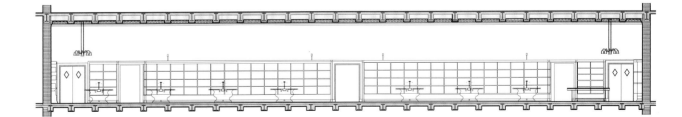

151

The elaborate wooden fixtures and fittings have now been restored and improved – in the case of the desks, to accommodate better lighting and more space for laptops and other study materials.

The David Reading Room

The David Reading Room is at the very top of the building in the space formerly occupied by the top of the original central bookstack, and therefore affords wonderful views of Oxford's 'dreaming spires' to the south, and the greenery of Trinity College gardens to the north. The room is structured as a steel frame perched on top of the newly constructed concrete upper stack.

The proportions of the perimeter shelving and panelling to the room have been carefully designed to respond to the privileged views out, and to make the most of the available space and volume.

The vertical strips of linear glazing arranged in rows on both the north and south sides of the building are signature Scott features, and key to the building's mid-twentieth-century architectural character. On the south side the shelving is full height to either side of each window, but it chamfers in plan to allow more natural light in and increased oblique views out. On the north side, the module of the shelving and panelling is also narrow, but is broken up by two large windows which relate directly to the north glazing strips. These narrower modules on the north and south sides create an increased sense of height within the room, while a wider module to the east and west ends helps to increase perceived width and volume. All of the joinery is of European oak with a dark stain to contrast with the varied colours of the book spines.

Three new triple-glazed roof-lights provide diffused natural light onto the working plane, and prevent ultra-violet and direct sunlight from harming the books. The ceiling is composed of three module widths of natural European oak slats, which align with a 'bronzed' pelmet detail around the perimeter of the roof-lights. New readers' tables have been arranged symmetrically either side of the east–west axis, with the reserve desk located at the west end of this axis. Through this careful attention to proportions, materiality and light in the design of this room, we achieved a richness of spatial and acoustic quality, and an atmosphere of quiet scholarly gravitas.

The east core on this level also provides managed access to a new roof terrace via a glazed link bridge within the high-level void on the east side of Blackwell Hall. This roof terrace has unique views across to the Sheldonian Theatre and Clarendon Building, and the older buildings of the Bodleian complex beyond.

Revealed by the removal of the Indian Institute extension, the south elevation of the newly created David Reading Room is punched by Scott's trademark vertical slot windows. Specially designed open access bookshelves sit between each of the openings.

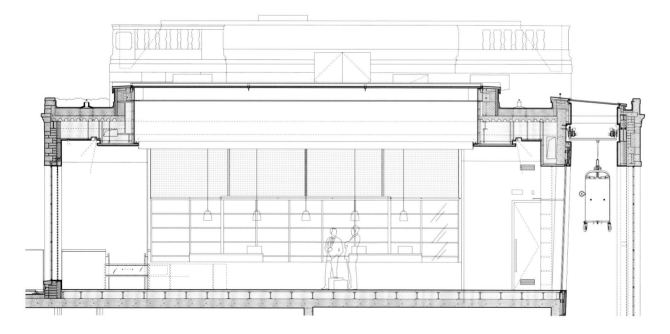

Long and cross sectional drawings of the David Reading Room, showing access to the main study space.

Overleaf:
The finished room is given warmth with a deep-toned timber soffit and panelling.

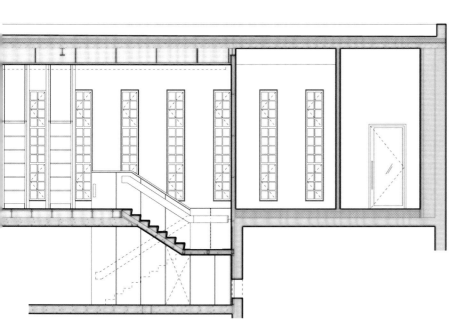

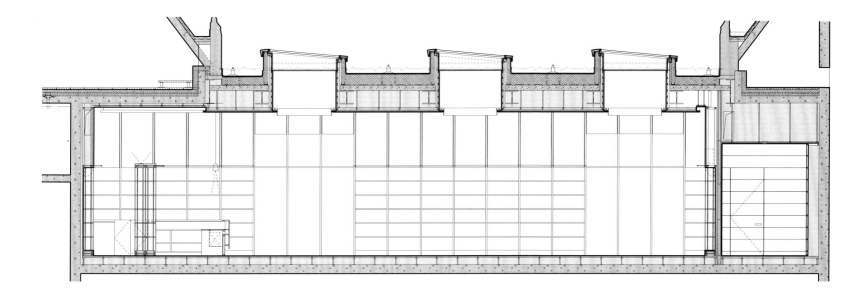

Scott's signature: the slender vertical slot windows frame views out towards the Oxford skyline, and stand in rank along one side of the external terrace at rooftop level.

Overleaf:
The view from the terrace offers a unique perspective of the city and, in particular, the Bodleian complex. The Clarendon Building and Sheldonian sit in the foreground, framed by the spires of the Old Bodleian and the dome of the Radcliffe Camera beyond.

Reconstructing the New Bodleian
Keith Vance

Build and demolition: the gradual transformation – and reveal – of Scott's building.

Overleaf:
The huge crane became a familiar sight as construction progressed, nicknamed 'Big Red' by the locals and 'Bodzilla' by library staff. In this view, the original bookstack structure has been fully removed, and work begun to pour concrete for the new floors.

There are many words that can be used to describe Sir Giles Gilbert Scott's New Bodleian Library. It is imposing? Yes. Iconic? Certainly. Haunted? Probably ... Straightforward? Never. A building that was built to last a hundred years and which survived the threat of war was not going to allow a group of builders in steel toe-capped boots and high-visibility vests to remodel sections of it without a fight. At first glance, the task did not look that imposing: a year to knock the central section down, a year to rebuild it, and a final year to fit it out. But each of these three phases of the project has presented its own challenges and rewards.

The demolition phase effectively involved the removal of the whole of the centre of the building – the main bookstack – leaving the retained, listed perimeter *in situ*, almost like a giant doughnut. What we hadn't really appreciated was the robustness of the original construction and the materials used. When demolition started, our first task was to strip out all the metalwork and commence removal of that 1930s wonder substance – asbestos. In all, we removed 80 tonnes of asbestos and 1,000 tonnes of steel and this revealed some interesting finds. We discovered, when removing the old library shelving, that when those early twentieth-century construction workers smoked, they smoked a lot. We found close to one hundred old cigarette packets, many of them still complete with the cards that everyone used to collect. We also unearthed pieces of crumpled brown paper which, when teased open, turned out to be the sandwich bags in which the workers must have carried their lunches. Many of these carried advertisements for sandwich shops and butchers across Oxford which have long since closed. Many of our finds are now housed in the Bodleian's Johnson Collection which preserves social records of the time.

Another early task during the demolition was the removal of the 1960s Indian Institute building from the roof, exposing the original roofscape and structure for the first time in fifty years. Once this had been carried out, we were able to remove the existing stone facade, enabling its reinstatement later in the build, exactly as Scott originally intended it. Each piece was individually numbered and stored to ensure its exact reinstatement.

Due to the constrained nature of the site in the city centre, the logistics were complex. There was only one road that could be used for removal of the demolition waste. Unfortunately, during the construction of the original building, no-one anticipated that refurbishment works of this nature would ever be carried out, and so the road running over the basement had a weight limit of just over eight tonnes. We needed it to take twenty-tonne skips. But we had, of course, planned for this and installed a huge temporary backpropping scheme, which transferred the load through three storeys of basement to the new slab level. Whilst demolition was being carried out on the upper floors, in the basement we were removing the conveyor system which moved books from the New Bodleian to the older library buildings on the opposite side of the road via a tunnel beneath Broad Street. One section of this has been retained and will be rebuilt in the basement as a relic of this ingenious system.

To facilitate the demolition, and later the construction, a tower crane was required. The only location for the crane that would not impede future phases of work was the retained perimeter of the building, and to minimize its impact, as small a hole as possible had to be cut through the structure. The exercise was not unlike threading a needle, and the installation of the crane drew crowds of tourists and locals. The crane towered over the neighbouring buildings and remained *in situ* for two years. It became a landmark in its own right and was nicknamed 'Big Red' by the locals. One of the highlights of the tours we organized for the Bodleian librarians was standing at the base of Big Red to see the seventy tonnes of concrete that held it in place. Once we had demolished the central stack to the lowest basement level, we had the pleasure of taking Bodley's Librarian[1] Sarah Thomas and her colleagues from across the library into the basement where, for the first time since the library was constructed, they could see up through the building to the sky eleven storeys above them.

It was decided for structural reasons that the lowest level basement slab had to be removed and replaced. While not a difficult task in itself, it came as an unwelcome surprise to discover that none of the steel columns holding up the building had been bolted down in the original works and simply relied

A sequence of drawings by the main contractors, Mace, shows the construction timeline.

In the first stage of demolition works (left top), the tower crane is erected and the retained facades supported.

During the second stage (left bottom), the central bookstack is carefully demolished, and the now-exposed facades of the perimeter accommodation protected with cementitious board.

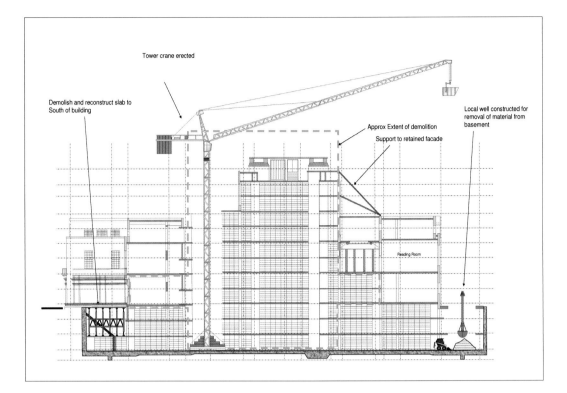

Tower crane erected

Demolish and reconstruct slab to South of building

Approx Extent of demolition

Support to retained facade

Local well constructed for removal of material from basement

Reading Room

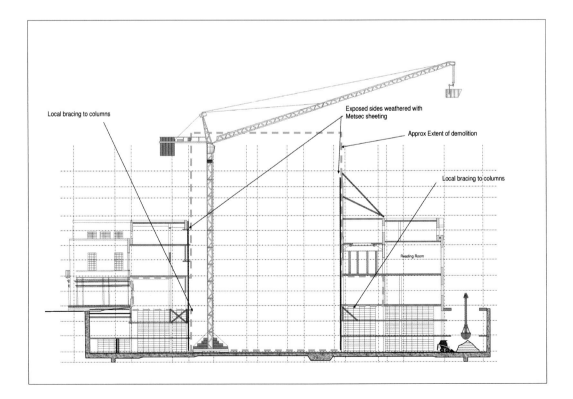

Local bracing to columns

Exposed sides weathered with Metsec sheeting

Approx Extent of demolition

Local bracing to columns

Reading Room

Props and temporary staging are then put into place to allow the steelwork – and subsequently the formwork – to begin.

Finally, the new racking is fitted in the basement, the hanging structures added above the Blackwell Hall and the high level steelwork installed to close up the atrium.

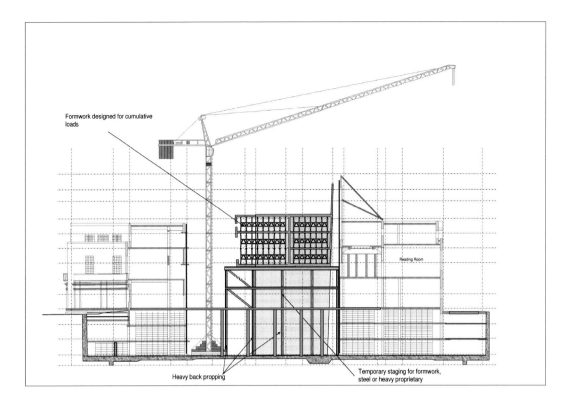

Formwork designed for cumulative loads

Reading Room

Heavy back propping

Temporary staging for formwork, steel or heavy proprietary

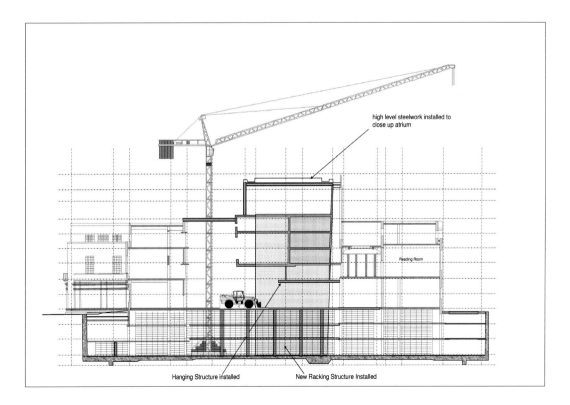

high level steelwork installed to close up atrium

Reading Room

Hanging Structure installed

New Racking Structure Installed

upon the slab to retain them. This left us with a building that was, in effect, freestanding. There was then an intense burst of activity bolting down all the columns to ensure that the building remained standing.

One of the most significant undertakings of the demolition phase was the uncovering of the roof-lights in Reading Room One. We had assumed that these roof-lights had been covered up some time post-construction because they had started to leak, but we discovered that they had in fact been covered with incendiary-proof concrete shortly after the building was completed during World War II. Their reinstatement means that for the first time ever, the reading room will have natural lighting, just as Scott envisaged.

Once the construction phase had started our main concern was to construct the two cores, east and west, as quickly as possible. To do this, we used jump forming techniques – casting the concrete in a series of vertical sections called 'lifts' – on both stacks simultaneously to create the appearance of a floating stack above the main ground floor space. Once this was complete, we used Big Red to lift in the 23-metre-long, 12.2-tonne roof beam, along with the two link bridges which tie the new and retained sections of the building together. Whilst all this was under way, the installation of building services had begun in the basement levels. One of the primary goals of the project was – as mentioned elsewhere – to install building services to enable the Bodleian to comply with BS 5454:2000, the British Standard for the storage of archive material. The installation of these services into a basement with a floor-to-ceiling height of just over two metres has been likened to fitting a pair of size eleven site boots into a size five shoebox. New, low-velocity ventilation had to be introduced to achieve the correct temperature and humidity for the storage of fragile books, together with a lighting system which minimized ultra-violet radiation upon these books. Due to the limited heights of the basement floors and the close spacing of columns, we were limited in what we could bring down through the building in prefabricated sections, so the systems have been installed on site by hand, piece by piece, exactly as they would have been when the building was originally constructed.

The third and final stage of the project – the fit-out works – also presented many interesting challenges. Not only did we have to get Scott's original wooden chandeliers refurbished for the main reading room, we also had to find a company which could manufacture two identical copies to replace those removed during the 1960s. All the existing doors and clocks, including two wooden and one stone clock, have been retained, refurbished and reinstalled. Original plasterwork has had to be repaired and some sections reinstated to match the existing material. The university's joinery team has worked with us to sensitively repair and replicate the 1930s bookshelves, returning the reading rooms to their former glory.

So, at the end of a project which has taken three years and involved 2,000 workers, what are we most proud of? One of our greatest achievements is to have carried out this complex demolition and reconstruction project without a single reportable injury in nearly a million man hours of work. We have rebuilt the structure so that, for the first time ever, the public will be able to enter and marvel at some of the awe-inspiring documents kept by the Bodleian Library. Importantly, we have achieved all of this without upsetting the neighbours: Blackwell's Bookshop, Trinity College and the Sheldonian Theatre. We have also worked closely with Oxford City Council and their highways team to minimize the effect of our works on one of Oxford's busiest, most filmed and attractive streets. Under the Construction Youth Trust's 'Budding Brunels' scheme, we have given young students who are interested in becoming part of the construction industry work experience on a live site. And every worker on the site says that they will bring their families to visit the building once it is open: such is their pride in it. We all agree that a job like the New Bodleian only comes along once in a lifetime. Is the library ghost happy? We hope so. As he or she wanders around the three basement levels containing thirty-five kilometres of new shelving and millions of books, we'll hope we have restored a national treasure to its rightful place.

[1] Bodley's Librarian is the head of the Bodleian Library, named after the institution's founder Sir Thomas Bodley. This post was held by Sarah Thomas until 2014, when she was replaced by Richard Ovenden.

As the old Indian Institute extension was removed, and Scott's slot windows reinstated, new views began to emerge across the city to the south.

Details

Materials and detailing in the Weston Library
Geoff Turner

Scott's Gesamtkunstwerk

One of the most striking features of the original New Bodleian Library building is the totality of Scott's design, which he envisioned as a *gesamtkunstwerk*, or complete work of art. His attention to detail meant that he not only managed the selection of quality materials such as stone, aluminium, bronze, steel, plaster and timber, but also designed door knobs and handles, furniture and light fittings, reading tables and chairs. As architects of the renewed building we were therefore responsible for retaining the coherence of Scott's vision, extending his palette of materials to ensure that the contemporary detailing would sit comfortably alongside, and complement, the old.

Stonework

Scott used three types of limestone throughout the building: Bladon and Clipsham externally and Taynton for the internal finishes. Bladon is a local Oxfordshire stone, with varying sized blocks (known as 'rubble') laid in loose courses and the surface roughly finished by hammer (or 'hammer dressed') for the broad expanses of external walling. The Clipsham ashlar, used on many buildings in Oxford, was sourced from a little further afield in Rutland, and at the New Bodleian was used for both the detailed mouldings and carvings, and for the stone dressings with a 'bush-hammered', textured finish.

All of the original stone removed from the south facade was salvaged, and either reused during the reconstruction of the upper stack facade, or reworked to form the ground floor columns. Where needed, new Clipsham stone was sourced from the same quarry as the original. The original external stones were cleaned with a non-aggressive water-based solution and repaired where necessary. Particular attention was paid to the two angels which hold the university's coat of arms on the east facade, the bust of Sir Thomas Bodley above the King George VI door at the south-east corner, and each of the unique cartouches above the bays on the south facade.

Taynton stone was used by Scott throughout the interior of the building: as a dado to all corridors and stairs; for the columns, capitals and frieze in the original Catalogue Room; and for the cladding and detailing to the whole of the Parks Road entrance lobby and corridor. Taynton is a coarse-grained oolitic limestone from Oxfordshire, which is naturally buff to white in colour, and has abundant shell fragments and veined stripes. Taynton can be seen in many Oxford buildings, including some of the detailing in the Divinity School, and gives a warm, rich effect, full of interest.

At the New Bodleian, Scott typically used the Taynton as a 20-millimetre-thick stone veneer, which was then 'tea-stained' to give it a richer buff colour. As much as possible of the Taynton was salvaged and reused, but this was not quite enough for the new dressings and architraves around the perimeter of the entrance hall. Unfortunately the original Taynton quarry is now closed, and so we sourced another oolitic limestone, Creeton, with similar visual and geological characteristics from Lincolnshire. Just as in the 1930s our stonemasons stained the Creeton to get a good match to the buff colour of the Taynton stone – this time using both tea and linseed oil to achieve the desired shade.

Great care had to be taken working with the Taynton stone due to the slim profile of the veneer and its attachment to the wall behind – a combination of plaster dab adhesion with wire fixings. This was especially the case during the demolition phase of the central stack, when the stack floor slabs were cut to separate them from the adjacent walls to minimize vibration through to the perimeter accommodation. All of the internal stone walls had to be carefully protected during such construction phases.

For the large expanse of pavement to the new Blackwell Hall on the ground floor of the building, we selected Jura Beige limestone, laid in three coursed widths and with varied lengths between 300 and 900 millimetres. We chose the stone for its light golden colour with plenty of variation, and its high shell content, which gives it a textured, fossil-like quality that sits well within the wider palette of Taynton stone, lime plaster and timber joinery. It is also a dense, hard stone, durable and hard-wearing in this heavily trafficked entrance hall and event space.

Cleaned stonework to the building's exterior, including the university coat of arms, and curved wall plinth.

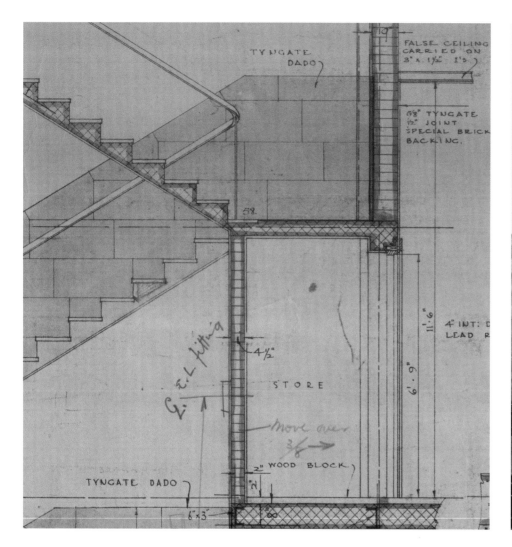

Detail of Scott's drawing showing the stone veneered dado to an internal stair, and an image of the refurbished original.

The light golden Jura Beige limestone used on the floor of the Blackwell Hall was selected from this quarry in Solnhofen, near Munich in Germany, for its hardness and durability. Its textured quality also contrasts well with the wider palette of Taynton stone, lime plaster and timber joinery.

Metalwork

Scott was always keen to embrace and pioneer modern building techniques, and this is evidenced at the New Bodleian in the windows, which represent the first large-scale use of aluminium in the UK. As no contractor had ever refurbished seventy-year-old aluminium before, we gained advice from a specialist consultant as to how exactly it should be done.

A couple of windows which were not required for reuse were used for a series of trials to determine the best cleaning and refurbishment technique. A basic, non-abrasive and neutral clean was carried out to remove surface dirt and grease. Elcometer readings identified that the existing anodized aluminium was generally in good condition, with the micron thickness only degrading locally in damaged or extremely weathered areas. In fact, the quality of the aluminium was so good that the micron thicknesses recorded on the seventy-year-old aluminium were very similar to what you would expect to find on new anodized aluminium. We carried out extensive research into possible protective finishes, but due to the quality of the existing aluminium, and the unknown effect a new coating might have on it over the long term, we only applied a protective finish to those areas of aluminium that were particularly damaged, such as those windows adjacent to an exhaust flue.

The ground and first floor windows were internally beaded and had therefore survived well, but the windows to the second floor and above were internally puttied and this had degraded badly. Where reglazing was necessary to these upper-level windows, the putty was removed and new glass installed – either 4-millimetre clear sheet glass, 9-millimetre Slimlite gas-filled double glazing units, or 7-millimetre UV barrier glass, depending upon the location of the window. A new aluminium glazing bead was set back from the internal leading edge of the original T-section profile of the mullion and transom to create a coherent reinterpretation of the original Scott design aesthetic. Other Scott-designed metalwork elements within the building, such as the bronze screen and doors and lower roof-light frame to the former Catalogue Room, perimeter fanlights, and the painted steel-and-glass doors to each of the four perimeter stairs, follow a similar architectural language of detailing: that of a series of twin metal flats, or recesses with back-to-back metal angles. This arrangement is very similar to the metal angle glazing bead detail seen on Scott's classic K2 red telephone box.

The original ornate balustrades to the four perimeter stairs are metal painted with gilt-bronze paint. The metal and glazed screens and doors to either end of the Mackerras Reading Room are bronze but are treated with the same original gilt-bronze paint to create a patina of age. Both these elements have had a light-touch clean as part of the refurbishment.

It is within the context of Scott's distinctive architectural language that we then designed all new-build metalwork elements both inside and outside the building. Recessed metal detailing, twin flats and back-to-back angles have been incorporated into all new internal metal and glazed screens, partitions and doors, the exposed structural steelwork, the external colonnade glazed screen, the exposed mullions of the new roof-lights, wayfinding signage elements and desk counters.

Throughout the building, either a bronze or bronze-effect metal finish has been used on the metalwork to coordinate with the rest of the material palette. For those elements in public and reader access areas, which will come into regular contact with visitors, we have used either burnished brass (for framing elements) or a gilded metal with an antique bronzed and waxed finish (for furniture elements). Over time these materials will cope with wear and tear, scratches and dents much better than bronze, and the material will improve with age as the patina develops. We also used a dark, bronze-effect polyester powder-coated metallic finish to other internal metalwork elements.

Original Scott drawing showing the various singled-glazed, metal-framed windows which were used throughout the building.

Details of restored windows in the general enquiries area and to the east facade of the building.

The glazed bronze screen to the Mackerras Reading Room is one of the most significant pieces of original metalwork to be revealed by the refurbishment. The architectural ironmongery to the screen doors is particularly beautiful, with the door handles detailed by Scott as part of his *gesamtkunstwerk* (top left). Original door furniture elsewhere in the building has also been restored.

Plasterwork

The original lime plasterwork throughout the building is a natural buff colour with a rough-cast felt float finish. Unfortunately, in many locations the original finish had been painted over, but there were still several corridors and stairwells where the natural colour was visible. A specialist lime plaster subcontractor was appointed to carry out all the cleaning and repairs to the heritage plaster, and also for the application of new lime plaster. The first tasks were to analyse a sample of the existing lime plaster to determine the exact constituent ingredients, and to wash down the original plasterwork using clean warm water and sugar soap.

Our analysis helped us to formulate a recipe for the new lime plaster which was a close match to the original for repairs and chases. However, due to the breathability of the plaster, joints between new and old will always be slightly visible, and the more you try to work it in, the smoother the plaster becomes and more visibly different from the rougher felt float finish. After trialling several samples of both limewash and bound distemper at varying dilutions and pigments, it was agreed that a mild distemper would be used. This is a traditional approach which allows the lime plaster to breathe, and has the visual effect that the new and old appear to be unpainted but are seamlessly blended by the distemper wash across both.

To the three-storey walls around the perimeter of the entrance hall, we applied new lime plaster with a similarly textured felt float finish to the original walls. Several samples of plaster using different pigments were tested, and a warm, creamy buff tone, which is lighter than the original, was selected. This complements the tones of the adjacent timber and stone without being too dominant within the space.

The new lime plaster to the void space of the Blackwell Hall (right) has a warm, creamy texture, in gentle contrast to the original heritage plaster elsewhere in the building (left).

Joinery and furniture

The former Commonwealth Reading Room (now the Rare Books and Manuscripts Reading Room) was the best-preserved interior in the building. The wooden ceiling, chandeliers, shelves and clock have been restored, while the original readers' and invigilation desks have been extended and improved to suit changing research needs.

Throughout the building most of the joinery is sapele wood. Original doors have a grained timber veneer of figured or fiddle-back sapele framed with an exposed sapele lipping on all sides. The reveals, architraves and skirtings are also of sapele but with a solid, straight grain.

The tour de force of original joinery is the first floor main Rare Books and Manuscripts Reading Room, which has sapele bookcases and reading desks, an invigilation desk with double-curved timber fronts, geometric wood chandeliers, sunburst-style clocks, and an inlaid wood ceiling which mimics Native American or African designs in a stylized art deco manner. It is understood that the various types of wood in the ceiling were gathered from different parts of the British Commonwealth at the time of construction. Scott's 'total design' was carried through into other joinery elements such as office furniture, office tables, readers' tables and readers' chairs.

It was only possible to sustainably source small quantities of sapele timber to match the original and these were used primarily for replacements and repairs to the original sapele.

Samples of varnish coatings were removed from a stairwell handrail, timber doors, library desks, bookcases and door architraves, and were analysed using Fourier transform infrared spectroscopy (FTIR) to determine the precise nature of the original varnish and any subsequent applications.

All of the samples we examined displayed an identical chronology of varnish application, starting with the original varnish, a polyurethane coating first patented in 1937. Scott was always interested in new techniques and this would seem to fit in with the construction chronology as the building was completed in 1939. The next layer of varnish, a cellulose, acetate-based coating, was applied at an unknown later date.

The heritage joinery elements were refurbished using traditional materials and finishing techniques so, for example, the inlaid timber ceiling to the first-floor north reading room was cleaned using a sugar soap solution. Water damage was made good with a mild bleaching agent solution which removed stains without affecting the colours of the timber, and then a de-waxed shellac polish was applied before a final coat of satin polish.

Scott's original joinery was carefully designed and crafted to create a pleasing and harmonious whole, and similar care and attention was taken over the design, specification and detailing of new wooden elements to ensure that they sit appropriately alongside the originals. This was particularly important in the case of the elements that readers will come into contact with on a daily basis, as these small touches can make a considerable difference to the overall user experience of the library. These include the new timber shelving in the reading rooms and seminar rooms, reading room tables, study carrels, storage walls, lecterns, and information, enquiries and reserve desks.

Modern-day academic research using rare books and manuscripts typically requires sufficient desk space for a foam cradle, the book or manuscript itself, associated books and materials, task lighting, a laptop and power source, and a note pad. In dialogue with the Bodleian, the approximate size of table needed was calculated and then layouts tested in each of the reading rooms based on research materials likely to be consulted, and the size and orientation of the room. We then developed a detailed design for the desks which consisted of timber end panels, a solid timber edge to the top (with a scallop to coordinate with bespoke chairs), an inlay of desktop linoleum with a brass strip separating each reader's seat, a central band of gilding metal with flaps hiding power sources, and a linear light bar. Material samples for the timber, linoleum, gilding metal and lighting bar were reviewed and approved, and then the physical sizes of the tables mocked up in MDF. Detailed consultations with library staff helped to finalize the actual size, and ensure that the tables were not so big that the power flap was inaccessible. A similar level of consultation, design, model-making, sample review, mocking-up and prototyping took place prior to the manufacture of all the joinery elements that users touch and feel, including the commissioning of a new readers' chair, which is described elsewhere in this book (see page 192).

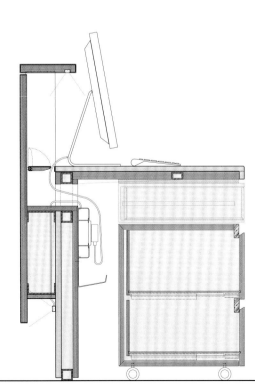

The information desk, which sits in the Blackwell Hall at ground floor level, is partially clad in Jura Beige limestone to match the floor finish. The countertop, which has a waxed bronze finish, is designed as a contrasting panel which 'floats' proud of the monolithic stone base.

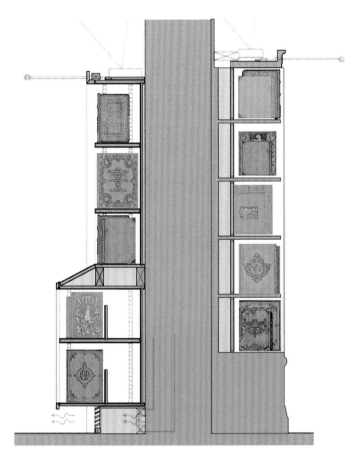

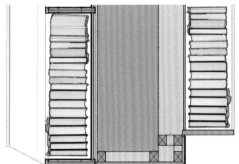

The perimeter shelving in the Mackerras Reading Room was designed in European oak with a similar profile to the original shelving, with a lipped slope on which to rest books, and open access shelves above and below. Diffuser grilles are integrated into the skirtings below, allowing cooled air to be delivered into the room from the conditioning system.

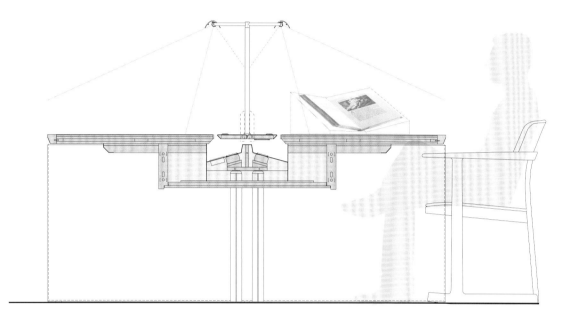

In the Mackerras and David Reading Rooms, new bespoke tables were designed in close collaboration with the Bodleian. The resulting tables have a slim, linear lighting bar which illuminates a linoleum desktop with a European oak edging. Light switches, data and power sockets are concealed beneath a bronzed metal flap within the central zone of the table.

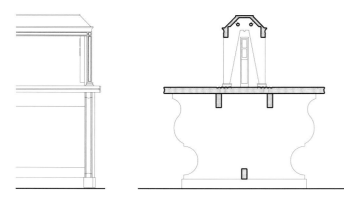
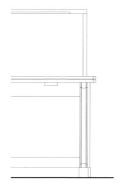
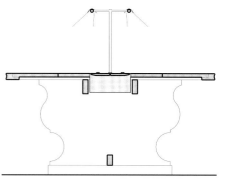

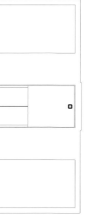

The original reading tables designed by Scott had a vertical hood dividing one side of the table from the other, which obscured invigilation sight lines across the reading rooms. Their shallow depth was also inadequate for modern research practice, with most readers requiring space for a laptop, while the fluting on the horizontal surface was potentially damaging to fragile manuscripts. The original tables were modified by removing the vertical hood and replacing it with task lighting with a slim profile. The fluting was also removed and, with the insertion of a central panel, the depth of the reader space increased by an extra 200 millimetres to each side of the table. Power and data access points have also been sensitively incorporated in a central zone, just as for the new tables shown opposite.

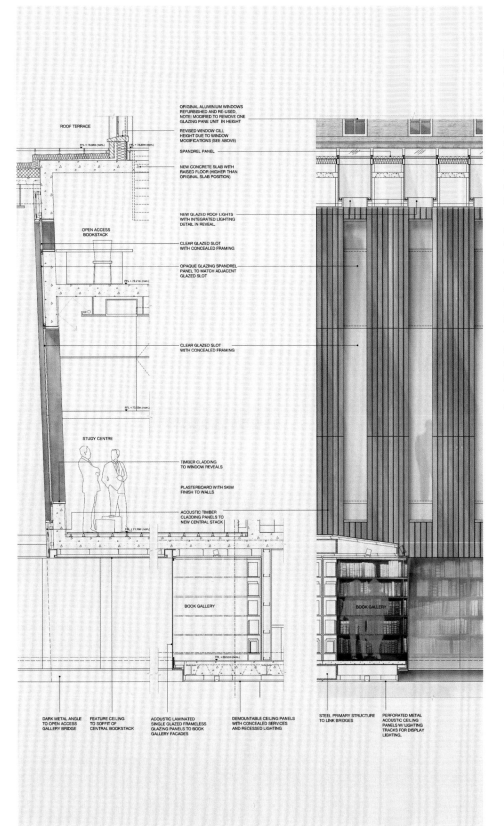

ROOF TERRACE

FFL + 78.89m (nom.)   FFL + 78.89m (nom.)

ORIGINAL ALUMINIUM WINDOWS
REFURBISHED AND RE-USED.
NOTE: MODIFIED TO REMOVE ONE
GLAZING PANE UNIT IN HEIGHT

REVISED WINDOW CILL
HEIGHT DUE TO WINDOW
MODIFICATIONS (SEE ABOVE)

SPANDREL PANEL

NEW CONCRETE SLAB WITH
RAISED FLOOR (HIGHER THAN
ORIGINAL SLAB POSITION)

OPEN ACCESS
BOOKSTACK

NEW GLAZED ROOF LIGHTS
WITH INTEGRATED LIGHTING
DETAIL IN REVEAL.

CLEAR GLAZED SLOT
WITH CONCEALED FRAMING

OPAQUE GLAZING SPANDREL
PANEL TO MATCH ADJACENT
GLAZED SLOT

FFL + 76.21m (nom.)

CLEAR GLAZED SLOT
WITH CONCEALED FRAMING

FFL + 73.53m (nom.)

STUDY CENTRE

TIMBER CLADDING
TO WINDOW REVEALS

PLASTERBOARD WITH SKIM
FINISH TO WALLS

ACOUSTIC TIMBER
CLADDING PANELS TO
NEW CENTRAL STACK

FFL + 71.18m (nom.)

BOOK GALLERY   BOOK GALLERY

FFL + 68.52m (nom.)

DARK METAL ANGLE
TO OPEN ACCESS
GALLERY BRIDGE

FEATURE CEILING
TO SOFFIT OF
CENTRAL BOOKSTACK

ACOUSTIC LAMINATED
SINGLE GLAZED FRAMELESS
GLAZING PANELS TO BOOK
GALLERY FACADES

DEMOUNTABLE CEILING PANELS
WITH CONCEALED SERVICES
AND RECESSED LIGHTING

STEEL PRIMARY STRUCTURE
TO LINK BRIDGES

PERFORATED METAL
ACOUSTIC CEILING
PANELS W/ LIGHTING
TRACKS FOR DISPLAY
LIGHTING.

Sustainably sourced European oak was used for face veneers and solid lippings to the new timber elements, with the grain directions quarter-cut slip-matched or crown-cut book-matched depending on their location and the purpose of the joinery. Three types of lacquer staining were applied to the timber finishes: a natural, light tone for new-build standalone areas such as the entrance hall; a mid-tone for those areas where the new European oak sits alongside original sapele; and a dark tone for those areas where we were particularly keen to ensure a strong visual contrast between the colour of the timber shelving and the spines of the books.

Coordination with the library's preventive conservators took place to agree a list of prohibited materials (such as those with volatile organic compounds) in book-sensitive areas. This was primarily for the secure bookstack areas, but also extended to the species of wood and varnish used in the reading rooms and seminar rooms. Although wood has the potential to emit acidity, it was agreed that in these rooms the ratio between the surface area of the timber finishes and the overall volume of the rooms was sufficiently low that the use of wood stains and lacquers was deemed acceptable. It was also agreed that these should be applied to the timber finishes well in advance of handover so that the finishes would be fully cured prior to the shelves coming into contact with books.

Detail drawing showing the subtly
canted timber wall of the Visiting
Scholars' Centre.

The light oak cladding of the Visiting
Scholars' Centre contrasts with the
texture and tone of the materials used
elsewhere in the Blackwell Hall.

The Bodleian chair
Barber Osgerby

In September 2012, the Bodleian invited designers and manufacturers to collaborate together in a competition to design a reader's chair for the Weston Library's new reading rooms. The intention was to create a new classic – a chair which would complement its surroundings and continue the library's history of commissioning bespoke furniture. As Professor Martin Roth, director of The Victoria and Albert Museum, and a competition judging panellist, commented, it should be 'a chair of chairs, for the library of libraries'.

The Bodleian's first commissioned chair was the historic curator's chair, a limited edition of twenty-eight made to a special design for the curators of the library in 1756, shortly after the opening of the Radcliffe Camera. The next redesign of the chair accompanied Scott's completion of the New Bodleian in 1936. He designed two seats for the building – one a bucket chair and the other straight-backed, both clad in heavy leather.

The third reader's chair, commissioned specifically for the new Weston Library, needed to be innovative and contemporary in design, and sit well within the new-build and refurbished spaces of the building, but it also needed to fulfil the Bodleian readers' very specific functional requirements. Most important among these was that it needed to be comfortable and supportive, allowing readers to sit for extended periods of time without discomfort, and appropriate to scholarly usage across a range of differing research formats and user behaviour. It must be simple (and silent) to use, and ergonomically flexible.

After receiving over sixty entries at the first stage of the competition, six teams were selected for a second stage, during which they developed initial designs to meet the requirements for comfort, practicality, longevity and character. These six designs were then reviewed and a shortlist of three partnerships selected to create a full-scale working prototype which could be tested by readers within a library environment.

In September 2013, a chair designed by Edward Barber OBE and Jay Osgerby OBE with manufacturer Isokon Plus was judged as winner of the competition. Their three-legged oak chair is a contemporary response to the brief and, with its sculptural form, has a strong sense of craft heritage as well as meeting the complex set of reader requirements. In Richard Ovenden's words, the chair 'is characterized by a strong identity, creative approach, comfort and suitability for intense study and research'.

The reader's chair exemplifies Barber Osgerby's deeply researched and intellectual approach to design. Early inspiration came from their strong local knowledge of the Bodleian – Jay Osgerby grew up around Oxford – and a shared admiration of the architectural and cultural impact of the Bodleian Library on the city. The designers also drew from research they had undertaken for previous chair designs, most notably the Tip Ton chair for Vitra.

They identified the rear view of the chair as critical to the concept of the design, as this is the most visible aspect when the chair is in situ. A strong vertical timber, resembling the spines of books on shelves, forms one of the three legs that attaches to the sled base. The generous rounded form of the seat frame is shaped to work for most variations in physique, and is echoed in both the sled base and the wide, supportive armrest which is ideal for use with notebooks and tablets. This circular form produces a strong and comfortable, yet remarkably light, oak chair. The upholstered seat has an elasticated webbing construction for support, with an additional foam layer for improved comfort. The forward tilt allows for a range of seating positions without the need for a complex mechanism.

The chair has been manufactured by Isokon Plus in the UK and, in line with the university's requirement that it should be sustainable in both material and construction, uses European oak and leather from a British tannery.

Initial sketches for the chair, showing
the development of the form. The
rounded, enclosing shape of the arms
remains a given, while various ideas
for the cross-bracing and arm
supports at either side are explored.

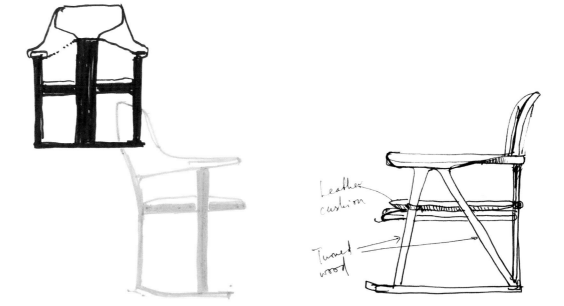

Leather
cushion

Turned
wood

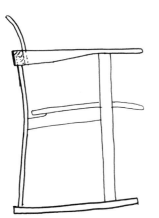

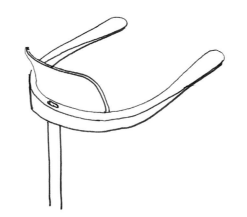

The development of a prototype chair was an integral part of the design competition process, allowing the shortlisted designs to be thoroughly tested. Once the Barber Osgerby design was selected, it went into production at the workshop of manufacturers Isokon Plus.

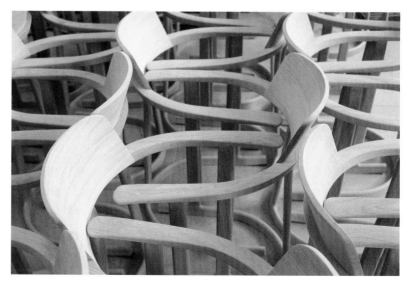

The completed chair, in response to a
brief which combined craft heritage, a
sculptural form and complex reader
requirements.

195

The chair in use, in the David Reading Room.

The Weston in use

What the users say

The Visiting Scholars' Centre is a completely new kind of space for the library. We have 18 fellowships that run from between one and nine months. They're intended to help people come to Oxford and carry out research in the Bodleian's Special Collections, and we host the fellows here in the Weston Library, alongside five who are on longer-term projects as part of the Centre for the Study of the Book. Each fellow has their own study, around a central seminar space. The central space in the VSC is very important in terms of sharing research information.

The Bodleian has unique collections, but it's also part of the wider university, so it needs to host research activity – and also academic events as a result of that research. We had aspired to do more of this in the past but couldn't live up to the aspiration. The building now has spaces to make this kind of interaction possible.

A core part of our activity is our work with students, with young people who are perhaps working on medieval texts but come here to look at the actual manuscripts. We are now able to schedule this kind of thing in every day. We have the seminar rooms to do it. With the students who come to visit, the emphasis is on the object. So much of the material they work from now is digitised, it can be quite a new experience for them to see the original objects. It's important for them to learn how to interact with physical books, because the original objects can enhance their learning. They get to see, for example, the extra notes added in the margins of books which aren't included in the digital texts.

Having seen the restoration, I've come to appreciate the building a lot. You can see how beautiful it is now. We've got great things in the collections and now we have the spaces to show them off. I've heard readers say that the reading rooms are conducive to good scholarship and that's not something I had heard before.

The exhibition room looks amazing and I'm thrilled about that. The exhibitions programme has always provided a great connection between the academics and the public, and I'm looking forward to that continuing with even better display possibilities.

I hated the way the building used to turn its back on Broad Street – it was just dead space. From the outside, I know people did feel excluded. That was a situation that some people were comfortable with. But that's all changed – we're trying to open the collections up now. The pendulum has swung.

Alexandra Franklin
Project co-ordinator, Centre for the Study of the Book

The Bodleian has a long history of showing its collections; not just books but also art, scientific objects and curiosities. When the Ashmolean Museum was established by the university many of the more 'artistic' objects were taken there, and over time others were transferred to the Museum of the History of Science and Pitt Rivers museums. But the Bodleian continued to exhibit its book and manuscript treasures in the reading rooms of the Old Library and for a while in the glorious setting of the Divinity School. Exhibitions were organised by library curators, experts in their field, but usually without training in museum practice to inform how collections should be looked after while on display. When the conservation department was set up in the 1970s, it began to have an involvement in the exhibitions and concerns over the harmful effects of light, temperature and humidity began to influence how material was displayed.

As the exhibition programme expanded a separate Exhibition Section was set up. Today there is a strong focus on public outreach, fund-raising, publication, academic collaboration and external partnerships. We want to demonstrate the impact of our collections – and conferences, lectures, masterclasses and, of course, exhibitions are a good way of engaging with the academic community and the public.

Our previous exhibition space off the Old Schools Quadrangle wasn't very visible. Now we're part of a beautiful, new public space in Oxford. There's a permanent treasures gallery and a temporary gallery for changing, themed exhibitions. In the temporary gallery the architects have designed airy, glass cases. These are permanent cases but they will still allow us to exhibit books and manuscripts in quite innovative ways because there's so much flexibility in the design. The project has even included the development of a new book cradle which carefully supports the book while it appears to hover in space like a butterfly.

We also have a work room adjacent to the galleries. This is a secure space with great environmental control and a huge central table. This is where the curators can come in to plan shows and do layouts, and we'll be able to gather the best ideas from everyone involved in an exhibition project; from the editors working on the exhibition catalogue to our colleagues designing merchandise for the shop. It's also where we'll be able to put items on cradles and prepare them for exhibition. One of the room's best features is a mock-up wall which replicates the display area of our exhibition cases. Essentially it's a case without the glass front. Not only will we be able to plan how to exhibit the collections, but it will also give us an opportunity to teach or work with student curators. It is a new beginning.

Maddy Slaven
Head of Exhibitions

A café animates Blackwell Hall, and serves as a new public meeting place in the heart of the city.

Books are now celebrated as objects throughout the library – in the display cases of the exhibition space and in the glazed run of open access bookshelves above Blackwell Hall.

The two exhibition galleries and lecture theatre are linked by the 'transept', which also provides additional space for digital interactives and the hanging of artwork – especially temporary displays of new acquisitions.

The east wall of the transept provides a display of the personal library of Basil Blackwell, known as 'the Gaffer'. The library was gifted to the Bodleian by Julian Blackwell, and marks a further link between the Bodleian and Blackwells.

The two exhibition galleries, ST Lee and the Treasury (the latter designed by Robin Partington Partners, and funded by the Helen Hamlyn Trust), provide contrasting display environments. The ST Lee gallery has been designed for changing, thematic exhibitions, whilst the Treasury is a 'jewel box' for some of the Bodleian's greatest treasures. Both galleries adopt a similar approach to case design, albeit with differing finishing details, and distinct floor and wall finishes and lighting design. Both galleries use purpose-designed support stands which make the books appear to 'float' – and this is especially evident in the Treasury.

The project has been revolutionary in terms of storage. Previously the map collections were stored underground in poor conditions. Health and safety was non-existent and the environmental conditions weren't ideal. Maps need a consistent temperature, and although the cabinets allowed us to store maps horizontally, they were far too full.

We have now moved everything to Swindon, and the bonus that we hadn't appreciated is that future storage – for the next century, in fact – has also been secured by us doing that. Our distance from the maps was a big issue at the start but we've adapted quickly. Ten per cent of the maps will come back to the Weston from Swindon as we fill out the stack, including the hand-drawn maps (which tend to be older and more vulnerable), and the heavy-use material.

There are three big map tables in the Rare Books and Manuscripts Reading Room, but we don't as yet have a dedicated map room in the new building. However, we do have a maps office next to the reading room. Previously we were in three different buildings.

The building's stunning now. It was dark and gloomy before, like an old station. It was intimidating to visitors. For me, the thing that delights me every time is when you pass one of the viewing areas into the old bookstack.

We were all so pleased to come back here – it's good to be all together again. We've been dispersed across the city, but the beauty is that there are all these experts here you can call on. The old team spirit has returned.

The Bodleian's been a deposit library for so long that its academic interest is multidisciplinary and completely global. So we've got a remit far beyond the university. I'm a huge fan of the public coming into the building. Before, there was nothing to say it was a library, but now we're going to be able to share our treasures. Once the front door's open, we're going to be able to welcome people in. It's going to be more visual and vibrant, more fit for purpose.

It's been a chance to rethink, in fact, in some ways it's been a rebirth. Staff are doing slightly different tasks, and mucking in. The playing field has been levelled somehow. It's been a good political move – an opportunity to iron out some of the inconsistencies in the way that we worked.

Nick Millea
Map Librarian

Conservation is by nature a compelling behind the scenes activity and our work strongly attracts the interest of both specialists in different areas and the general public. Our activities generate great philanthropic interest and, therefore, it is essential to be able to showcase our work in order to help Bodleian Libraries and the university as a whole to preserve our collections for future generations.

At the Bodleian, we have a leading conservation team of experts who have always been keen to share their knowledge. The Weston Library is an extraordinary vessel to help us achieve greater exposure, not only in situ in our state-of-the-art workshops, but also in the public areas of the building with our Samsung screens, which act as an open window to our day to day work. More than ever before, we are making an effort to satisfy the great demand from our own colleagues at the Bodleian and the university, from scholars and the general public to get closer to our work, and we are extremely fortunate to finally be able to achieve this in our wonderful new facilities.

Our projects range from small repairs which need minimal intervention, to very high profile projects that often take years to be completed. Having a purposely designed space to achieve our collection care goals through both the prevention of damage and the direct intervention on our treasures is paramount. We now have a large and flexible workshop where spontaneous learning has become part of our day to day environment. Additionally, we are now able to process deteriorated new acquisitions in our new quarantine room before they are sent to their permanent storage location. And we can even store our fragile photographic materials in a purposely built cool store.

With the Weston renovation, Bodleian Libraries are once more showing that we are an excellent conduit for people to access our collections in an environment that we are able to control, sustain and look after. Despite the unavoidable fact that every new building requires time to settle and reach optimal conditions, the new environmental control system is already helping us to manage temperature and relative humidity well in both the stack and in areas over ground.

Months after moving, I am still in awe because I come to work every day to this ecstatically beautiful building to which new light has been brought in, in more senses than just architecturally: there is a sense of happiness and pride in the people who work here, that translates into a greater sense of unity and much improved workflows. The building and its people are breathing in a much healthier way now. All of us who have been immensely lucky to be in the right place at the right time, being part of the making of the Weston Library, we know that this is an unprecedented opportunity for us to make a difference: I have no doubt that this is our moment.

Virginia M. Lladó-Buisán
Head of Conservation & Collection Care

The new third floor conservation workshops are airy, open-plan spaces. Despite the digitization of other parts of the library, highly specialist craft techniques are very much in evidence, with each member of staff working with a beautiful and personally curated set of tools, brushes, bowls and other objects. A still life of one such collection is shown on the opening pages to this section.

The original internal design of the stack was inspired by visits to the major libraries in the US. The fad of the time was to build in steel and concrete. The shelving was built around the dense steel framework, with each level divided by thin concrete floors which were thought to be fireproof. There was a gradual realization that building with steel and concrete wasn't necessarily fireproof. There were no fire suppression systems installed and the fire separation wasn't up to scratch, so the whole design needed a rethink.

The stack was a warren that took a good couple of months to learn, but once you knew the system you could find any book in minutes. We had a maximum of thirty people fetching and finding books, and feeding the machine (the Book Conveyor) to send and receive books through the tunnel in a continuous loop. You'd be stationed on a pair of floors, or a single floor depending on the time of year. It was a good place to work because we were quite a young staff. There was a rapid turnover of people but it had a good atmosphere, it was a very social place. I personally had a real interest in the material – you would see books from every discipline coming in.

I enjoyed being on the book-moving section because it meant you could really get close to the collections. We continually needed to move books around – the library had been underfunded during the 1950s, but the intake was close to a thousand new books a day, and they all needed cataloguing and processing. Now most go straight to Swindon, but at that time they were sorted into seven sizes, and then put into one of 300 major categories. Within each of those categories there were multiple subdivisions which defined the exact shelfmark. This meant that we had to keep many thousands of growth points open within the stacks so that there was room on the shelves for the new books. And the collections just kept on expanding. The whole history of the library revolves around lack of space and continual book moves.

There are twenty-one compartments in the new stack and we're about halfway through repopulating them. With the new stack, book delivery will be done entirely via trolleys and lifts. It will mean the staff are more mobile; less confined to the stack. We'll also have more interaction with the reading room staff. There'll be more trackability now, because there'll be a definite handover of the books. Some of the old camaraderie of the stack still exists, but now the building holds around a third of the amount of material it used to, and the numbers of stack staff have decreased accordingly. So, a million and a quarter items rather than three and a half million.

98 per cent of the collections are now in uniform archive boxes, so you no longer get quite the same experience of browsing among the open shelves. I used to enjoy that – I used to love seeing the thousands of specially-bound Jacobean plays for example. We've lost that experience, the smell of the books, but it's a very necessary measure in terms of conservation. We are looking after the collections in a more professional way, and they'll last longer.

This building hasn't been very well regarded in Oxford, but I've always liked it. I like Scott's style, his verticals. And the stack – for seventy years it did exactly what it was designed to do. I think WilkinsonEyre have done a fabulous job keeping the idea of his design, and yet opening up the spaces in new ways. The depth of Scott's work was hidden before, but now you can see what he was aiming for.

John Duffy
Assistant Projects Officer

The bookstack is still the quiet heart of the library, albeit with the collections now kept in improved archival conditions.

For many years the staff and services associated with Special Collections have been scattered – we've had some beautiful rooms but not a building which is ours. The new building allows us to fulfil our important traditional role of hosting researchers in reading rooms; but now we also have space to better store and catalogue collections, digitize them and promote them through exhibitions and events. We can draw academics and other researchers into special spaces such as the Visiting Scholars' Centre.

The configuration of space means that we should be able to develop and care for the collections and encourage research on them, but also welcome the public into the building. People are fascinated with the original object. These days, everyone is instantly connected to a shared pool of digital information. This cultivates a renewed interest in the experience of the real thing, a fascination with the materiality of the object. This building in some respects is an important anchor into the analogue – it's saying very clearly that we need to provide proper access to a tangible intellectual heritage. Seeing the object raises many questions that can't be investigated through the flat medium of digital.

There's great value in the digital too, of course, and massive potential to use it to bring new perspectives to our collections. The building has taken into account our need to collect and make accessible more digital material. We have spaces and staff to help with that, although we are only at the beginning of the challenge and we need to do more. Seeing how this new physical building interacts with the virtual world will be fascinating and we are already seeing some tantalising projects take shape.

What's the building like to work in? Before, it was very hard to read but now it's much more legible and friendly for staff, readers and, importantly, the public who never formed part of the original equation. By the time I arrived in Oxford in 2006 the building was a bit of a horror story. It had long out-served its original function and capacity and this project has given it a new focus and clarity of purpose. It's not a cliché to say it has been transformative.

Christopher Fletcher
Keeper of Special Collections

The university is full of very independent people, and using the library is one of the few group activities we do. It's a space for high-quality research, and that's our common ground. The conditions prior to the refurbishment were poor: the building had been abused. It was very dark, with blocked-up windows, and it was an unpleasant place to work. We knew it was unsafe, but it was also extremely cramped. The systems were antiquated, and it was often impossible to get everything you needed as a reader in one place and it was either boiling hot or freezing cold.

Now we've brilliant conditions. The feel of the building is substantial – it's not pinched. The desks and chairs have all been carefully considered, and the layout works well. It's a very inviting place to work. It's also a lot more organized in terms of retrieval, and the reorganisation of the book space for music is wonderful. The teaching spaces are feeling fairly busy, and it's clear to me that once the building's fully completed, our relationship as readers with the scholars will increase. It has has given us space to interact.

I like how the newer parts of the design have picked up on architectural cues in the existing building. The spaces are very uncluttered, and you don't feel overwhelmed with junk as we did before. The down-at-heel feeling has gone.

The Bodleian is special: it has things in its collections that exist nowhere else. The new library is more obviously a research centre, but it's become something that actively promotes its research activity. This has made the Bodleian more competitive.

The acknowledgement that the public want to see the library and its objects is very positive. This changing relationship between the Bodleian and its public is important. It makes the library feel welcome to people who want to discover it.

Michael Burden
Reader, Fellow in Music at New College, Professor in Opera Studies

Readers are now able to use more informal areas as well as the restored reading rooms, including the intimate oriel-style slot openings overlooking Blackwell Hall.

The public are able to view more informal displays in Blackwell Hall, as well as browsing in the Bodleian shop.

The opening

The Weston Library was officially opened to the public on 21 March 2015. More than 11,000 people visited the building over the first weekend.

The day before the public were welcomed in, two modern-day geniuses, Professor Stephen Hawking and Sir David Attenborough, visited the library to open the *Marks of Genius* exhibition, accompanied by Bodley's Librarian Richard Ovenden and other Bodleian staff, academics and friends.

Appendix

Professional teams

Project team
Architect	WilkinsonEyre
Project manager	Oxford University Estates Services and RBDML
Structural engineer	Pell Frischmann
Mechanical & electrical engineer	hurleypalmerflatt
Planning consultant	Turnberry Consulting
Fire engineer	Pell Frischmann
Cost consultant	EC Harris

Design consultants
Security	Consort Security
Specialist lighting	DHA
Art strategy	Modus Operandi
Fire suppression	Frontline Fire
AV consultants	Mark Johnson Consultants
Acoustics	Sandy Brown Associates
Visitor profile study	Morris Hargreaves McIntyre
Catering	Boyd-Thorpe Associates/Coverpoint
Catering design	IFSE
Wayfinding and signage	Holmes Wood

Contractors
Main contractor	Mace
Demolition	Keltbray
Logistics	Elliott Thomas
Sub- and superstructure	Byrne Bros
Mechanical & electrical design	Long & Partners
Stonework	Putney and Wood
Shelving	Forster Ecospace
Mechanical & electrical contractor	MJ Lonsdale
Commissioning	Dome Consulting
Fire	R&S Fire
Security	AIS
Specialist joinery	Opus Magnum
General joinery	Swift Crafted
Heritage joinery	OUES DLO
Glazing	OAG
Display showcases	Goppion
Flooring	AC Plc
Dry lining	Fireclad
Architectural metalwork	Delta Fabrications
Roofing	Imperial Roofing
Specialist plaster	Cook & Sons
Wayfinding and signage	Rivermeade
Lecture theatre seating	Figueros

Project data

Budget
£80.5 million

Spaces for readers
Three reading rooms (the Mackerras, the David and the Rare Books & Manuscripts Reading Rooms), providing 147 reader seats and 27 study carrels
Digital Media Centre with 15 seats
Visiting Scholars' Centre with 10 studies
2.5 km open access shelving off the reading rooms (850,000 volumes)
Four seminar rooms (total of 40 seats)
Staff and reader café with 38 seats
Admissions office and waiting area

Spaces for the public
The Bodleian café, with 76 seats
Lecture theatre with 119 seats
Two exhibition galleries
94 m² shop

Spaces for staff
Accommodation for over 200 staff and volunteers from the following service areas: Admissions, Bodleian Library of Commonwealth and Africa Studies at Rhodes House, Catering, Centre for the Study of the Book, Conservation & Collection Care, Exhibitions, Facilities Management, Imaging Services, Special Collections
Two workshops for conservation staff
Imaging studio
Ancillary storage areas
Staff common room

Spaces for the collections
39.5 km storage for rare books, manuscripts, archives, music, ephemera, maps over three basement levels
Secure archives processing area
Stack and other key areas protected by high-pressure water mist system
Compartmentalization of stack with four-hour fire walls
Strong room protected by gas suppression system
Extensive security systems throughout building using CCTV, access control and intruder detection systems
Building management system (BMS) controlling heating and ventilation (the collection storage areas are fully air-conditioned and held within bands of temperature and relative humidity in line with PD 5454)
Use of chilled beams in curatorial office areas to moderate temperature and humidity

Facts and figures

The New Bodleian Library

3.5 million	Number of items housed in the New Bodleian before it closed
11	Number of storeys in the original bookstack
1946	Year the building was first opened
2003	Year the building was accorded Grade II-listed status
70	Number of years the New Bodleian served its readers

Non-library activities in the New Bodleian during the Second World War

Inter-service topographical department of the Naval Intelligence Division
Naval War Library
Royal Observer Corps
Educational book scheme of the POW department of the British Red Cross and the Order of St John of Jerusalem
British Red Cross blood transfusion service
Slade School of Art painting studio
Basement used as a military base and partially converted into an air raid shelter for the city (although never used)
Safekeeping of some eighty deposits from libraries in London and elsewhere

Redevelopment and demolition

6,500 tonnes of concrete
80 tonnes of asbestos removed from the building
1,000 tonnes of steel
260 tonnes of general waste
140 tonnes of salvaged stone
81 km shelving removed from the stacks
3 km shelving removed from the reading rooms and offices
Over 1 million worker hours
12-month demolition phase
One 120-foot-high crane towering over the site
200 original aluminium windows refurbished
3,000 m² of flooring screed laid
45 metres of display boards (showing the Bodleian's treasures, A to Z) wrapped around the construction site

Items found during the demolition

WD & HO Wills' 'Capstan' Navy Cut cigarette packet; Smiths 'Quality' Californian Raisins packet; John Wiblin's Royal Oxford sausages paper bag; George VI pale red brown 1½D stamp; 'Imp' soap paper bag; Californian Poppy perfume card; Lovell's Liquorice Toffee Rex sweet wrapper; High Speed Twist Drill Bits paper packet containing seven drill bits; Vernons football pools coupons for 4 September 1954; Handwritten note containing address of POW camp in Italy; Receipt from Blackwell's for book purchased by Red Cross POW on 23 June 1942

Book moves

42 km of books moved into the Weston in total
14 km of books moved in from the temporary special collections stack in the Radcliffe Science Library
16 km of books moved in from the Book Storage Facility (BSF) at South Marston near Swindon
The moves started with the Rhodes House to BSF move on 21 January 2013, and finished with the BSF to Weston move, ending on 1 June 2016 – so the seven separate move projects lasted almost 3.5 years!

One of these was the open shelf moves, immediately before the opening of the reading rooms, which brought in books from six different locations
Approx. 500,000 volumes and boxes of special collections material located in the Weston

The Weston Library

42	km of shelving overall (equating to approximately 1,264,000 volumes, and including 39.5 km in basement archive and reserve areas for the special collections and 2.5 km of open access material in reading rooms and open access stacks)
60	Original Scott chairs refurbished (45 low-back armchairs and 15 easy chairs)
16–18°C	Ideal temperature for storing rare books
99	Number of CCTV cameras installed inside to offer security for the collections

Special collections

The Bodleian's special collections are divided into two main groups: Western Manuscripts & Rare Books, Maps and Music; and Oriental Manuscripts & Rare Books. Oxford University humanities theses also form part of the collections, as do university archives and the institution's own administrative records. Among the special collections are:

The largest collection of pre-1500 printed books in any university library, and the fifth largest collection of incunabula in any library in the world (5,623 editions in 6,755 copies).

A highly important collection of manuscripts from medieval Europe and the Byzantine Empire – the largest to be found in any university library in the world, and within the United Kingdom second only to the British Library.

The John Johnson Collection of Printed Ephemera: one of the most important collections of printed ephemera in the world, containing around 1.5 million items spanning from 1508 to 1939 (and beyond in some areas).

One of the largest concentrations of modern British political manuscripts and archives, drawn from the private papers of politicians from all three major political parties, as well as from public servants, print and broadcast journalists, and others active in public life. In scale the collections range in size from over 2,000 boxes to a single diary.

Unrivalled holdings centred on Percy Bysshe Shelley and Gerard Manley Hopkins. Substantial archives relating to J.R.R. Tolkien, C.S. Lewis, Charles Williams and other members of the Inklings circle. Its manuscript holdings for the modern period reflect the library's interest in acquiring papers of authors who have a connection with the university and city of Oxford.

Timeline

1925
Sir Arthur Cowley (Bodley's Librarian) warns about the future of the library's capacity

1930
Commission appointed under Sir Henry Miers to address capacity issue

1931
Sir Edmund Craster appointed as Bodley's Librarian

1931
Report on library provision in Oxford published and findings endorsed by Congregation

June 1934
Sir Giles Gilbert Scott appointed as architect

14–31 July 1934
European libraries tour by Craster and Scott

30 Aug–16 Oct 1934
US and Canadian libraries tour by Craster and Hill (Bodley's secretary)

April 1935
Second European libraries tour by Craster

10 June 1935
Instructions to the architect approved

December 1936
Building work begins

June 1937
Foundation stone laid by Queen Mary

March–June 1939
Conveyor installed

Summer 1940
The building is nearly finished, despite the outbreak of the Second World War

1941
Public bomb shelter built in basement

1940–45
The building is used for a number of war-related activities; at the same time 1.5 million books are moved in and library services maintained

24 October 1946
The building is opened by King George VI

1966–9
The Indian Institute extension is added at roof level

October 2003
New Bodleian Library becomes a Grade II-listed building

May 2006
Conservation statement published by heritage consultants Purcell

July 2006
WilkinsonEyre appointed as architects for the refurbishment following design competition

March 2007
US libraries tour by consultant team

September 2008
Confirmation of donations from the Weston Foundation and Blackwell

13 March 2009
The New Bodleian is renamed the Weston Library following a £25 million donation by the Garfield Weston Foundation

May 2010
Planning and listed buildings consent granted

November 2010
Book decant begins

April 2011
Mace appointed as main contractor

July 2011
Book decant complete

29 July 2011
The New Bodleian closes its doors after seventy years

August 2011
Demolition works begin

August 2012
Construction begins on superstructure

August 2013
Fit-out works begin

October 2014
Academic opening of the Weston Library

March 2015
Public opening of the Weston Library

Sustainability notes

The Bodleian Libraries' objectives of safeguarding the collections, modernizing research facilities and promoting the collections to the public all had an influence on the environmental sustainability of the project.

The renewal of an eighty-year-old building is in itself a sustainable solution: 88% of the original façade was retained, with another 150m² of non-original stone from the 1960s extension reused. In total, 140 tonnes of salvaged stone were reinstated. Although the building's Grade II listing and its location in a conservation area presented some constraints, the environmental strategy for the renewed building – just as the overall architectural design – is based around making the building work as hard as possible with only subtle interventions to the existing fabric. The strategy's key features are:

Reuse of the building envelope to reduce embodied energy throughout the build

Reuse and recycling of demolished material from the building

Use of the building's inherent thermal mass, including its fabric, contents, the new concrete bookstack, and its high thermal and hygroscopic characteristics to reduce temperature and humidity fluctuations

Maximization of natural daylighting where possible by reinstatement of roof-lights

Installation of new solar glass or solar film on existing windows to reduce unwanted solar gain and ultra-violet light

Specification of low u-values for all new-build elements

Specification of water-efficient plant, appliances and fittings

Replacement of existing electrode boilers with high efficiency gas-fired boilers

Installation of energy-efficient chiller system to minimize electrical consumption

Installation of energy-efficient recirculating ventilation system in bookstack

Strategy of heat recovery from condensers

Use of low-energy chilled/heated floor in Blackwell Hall

Installation of intelligent building management system

Use of solar thermal collectors to supplement hot water requirements – the only feasible source of renewable energy due to the site and building constraints

Specification of LED lighting where possible

Specification of hardwearing – and recyclable – natural materials for all internal finishes to achieve a long lifespan

Promotion of a green transport plan to take full advantage of good public transport links, and supported by improved cycle facilities

By their very nature, the bookstacks had to be environmentally serviced, due to the requirements of BS 5454, the existing floor-to-floor heights and the constraints imposed by the building's heritage status. However, this servicing was designed to be as energy-efficient as possible and it is estimated that, as a result, there has been a 13.6% reduction in energy consumption compared to the building before refurbishment, which represents a reduction in CO_2 emissions by 10.6%.

The scheme achieved a BREEAM rating of Very Good (in draft). An Excellent rating was not possible because of the constraints of the building's heritage listing and the narrow environmental control envelopes required to achieve BS 5454 archive standards in the bookstack areas.

Afterword

The completion of the Weston Library is highly significant in the context of the University of Oxford's wider estate. Scott's refurbished building sits within the geographic and academic heart of the city, and has symbolic importance as an intellectual treasury. But the project is also significant for the way in which an existing, historic building has been transformed into a place suitable for twenty-first century scholarship and public interface. The challenge of making some of the oldest buildings in the city useful and accessible for modern use is a fundamental concern for the university's estates team.

The University of Oxford's estate includes over two hundred and fifty buildings used for teaching, research and administration. It encompasses some of the finest buildings in the city of Oxford – the oldest dating from 1424 – and 25 per cent of it is listed. Almost every project, therefore, whether it is the rethinking of an existing building, or the construction of a new one, has to be considered against this rich architectural heritage.

The projects which work best are those which take advantage of, and build on, the innovation of past designers and architects; those which are uncompromisingly modern but which do not compromise the ancient and continually developing grain of the city. The Weston Library achieves this, with new and old elements coming together to create a building which is somehow more than the sum of these parts.

Mike Wigg
Former director of Capital Projects and Property Management at the University of Oxford

Contributor biographies

Robert Bevan

Robert Bevan is a journalist, heritage consultant and placemaker. He is former editor of *Building Design* and is now the *London Evening Standard*'s architecture critic. He has written for design, art and travel magazines around the world. His work aims to connect contemporary architecture and design with history and place.

Geoffrey Tyack

Geoffrey Tyack is a fellow of Kellogg College and director of the Stanford University Programme in Oxford. He is author of *Oxford: an Architectural Guide* (Oxford University Press, 1998), and recently co-edited a book on the work of the Victorian architect Sir George Gilbert Scott, grandfather of the New Bodleian's designer.

Michael Morrison

Michael Morrison is a partner of Purcell, heritage consultants to the Bodleian Library. He has worked on some of the most significant historic buildings in the UK, including the National Gallery and British Museum. He prepared the original conservation reports on Scott's New Bodleian, and has, with his team, continued to provide heritage advice to the project throughout its design and construction.

Richard Ovenden

Richard Ovenden was appointed as the University of Oxford's twenty-fifth Bodley's Librarian in 2014, taking on the stewardship of combined collections numbering more than 11 million printed items, in addition to 50,000 e-journals and a vast quantity of other materials. He was instrumental in developing a vision for the new Weston Library from 2004 as a centre for the highest quality scholarship, intellectual exchange and broader public access.

Toby Kirtley

Toby Kirtley is estates projects officer to the Bodleian Libraries, a post he has held since 2001. With a background in library preservation, he has been instrumental in a number of major capital projects across the library's estate. His work at the Weston Library as client representative has extended from developing the concept and business case, drawing up the brief, managing and enabling work such as the decant from the building, to the implementation of the project on site and the Weston's subsequent reoccupation.

Jim Eyre

Jim Eyre is a director and co-founder of WilkinsonEyre, and led the design of the Weston Library from its conception right through to completion. He was awarded an OBE for his services to architecture in 2003, and was the first architect to receive the Bodleian Library's highest accolade – the Bodley Medal – in 2015.

Geoff Turner

Geoff Turner is an associate director at WilkinsonEyre, and has been with the practice since 1997. He directed the architectural team for the Weston Library, leading the consultation process with users and managing the design coordination of the project on site throughout its construction.

Bernard Antieul

Bernard Antieul is programme director at Breathe Energy, a consultancy which creates innovative energy and carbon efficiency solutions for businesses. Prior to this, he was a director at environmental engineers hurleypalmerflatt for over six years, leading the development of the servicing strategy for the Weston Library among other large-scale projects.

Les Chapman

Les Chapman is technical director at Pell Frischmann, and has been with the practice since 1990. He directed the structural design team for the Weston Library until completion, following the retirement of Richard Lamb, a former divisional director at the company, who led the main phases of the structural design.

Keith Vance

Keith Vance is operations director at Mace, a post he has held for over six years. Based on site throughout the refurbishment of the New Bodleian, he has managed the delivery of all the services engineering packages for the project, developing an in-depth knowledge of the building, its fabric and its history.

Jay Osgerby

Internationally acclaimed designers Edward Barber and Jay Osgerby founded their London-based studio in 1996. Their diverse body of work spans industrial design, furniture, lighting and site-specific installations as well as limited edition pieces and public commissions such as the London 2012 Olympic Torch and a two-pound coin designed for the Royal Mint. In 2013 they won the competition to design a new readers' chair for the Bodleian Libraries.

Mike Wigg

Mike Wigg is former director of Capital Projects and Property Management within the Estates Services Department of the University of Oxford, a post he held for thirteen years. He recently set up his own consultancy, Apex Development Management, and continues to work with the university on a number of projects within the Oxford estate.

Emma Keyte

Emma Keyte, editor and project manager of this book, is former head of communications at WilkinsonEyre and worked on the original design competition for the Weston Library. Her independent consultancy, Free:, helps architectural practices to communicate their ideas through books and other creative content.

Thank you to

Donors
Garfield Weston Foundation
Oxford University Press

Dr Ebadollah Bahari
Julian Blackwell
Antonio and Patricia
  Bonchristiano
George and Charles David
Dunard Fund UK
Manuela Campedelli Garuti
Helen Hamlyn Trust
The Headley Trust
Dr Lee Seng Tee
Andrew W. Mellon Foundation
The Zvi and Ofra Meitar Family
  Fund
The Polonsky Foundation
Samsung
Dr Joseph Sassoon
William and Judith Scheide
Douglas Smith
Dr André Stern
George W. Von Mallinckrodt
Barrie and Deedee Wigmore
Winston Wong

And many other generous
supporters

Development
Sue Cunningham
Jon Dellandrea
Liesl Elder
Elaina Gallagher
Tamsin Haigh
Lois Hargrave
Kristine Knox
Nick Rawlins
Amy Trotter

Project Sponsor Group
Prof Bill Macmillan
Prof Ewan McKendrick
Prof Ian Walmsley
Prof Vincent Gillespie
Prof Nicholas Cronk
Bryan Ward Perkins

Estates services
Bob Barbour
Denis O'Driscoll
Mike Wigg
David Oakey

Bodleian Libraries
Stuart Ackland
Edward Adcock
James Allan
Anneke Bambery
Roddy Bedford
Catriona Cannon
Jenny Chilcott
Vanessa Corrick
Sandrine Decoux
John A. Duffy
Gillian Evison
Chris Fletcher
Alexandra Franklin
Nicole Gilroy
Colin Harris
Shirin Hine
Martin Holmes
Andrew Honey
Laura How
David Howell
Michael Hughes
Clive Hurst
Martin Kauffmann
Ashleigh King
Mike King
Toby Kirtley
Virginia Lladó-Buisán
Andrew Macduff
Nick Millea
Robert Minte
Wilma Minty
Alice Ogilvie
Teresa Pedroso
Mark Revell
Boyd Rodger
Suzanne de la Rosa
Kristie Short-Traxler
Madeline Slaven
Victoria Stanbury
Sarah Thomas
Susan Thomas
Sarah Wheale
Helen Wilton-Godberfforde

Institutions and groups
Blackwell's Bookshop
The Broad Street
  Planning Group
The Friends of Broad
  Street
Oxford Civic Society
Oxford Preservation Trust
Oxfordshire Buildings
  Trust
Shepley, Bullfinch, Richardson,
  Abott
Trinity College, Oxford
Twentieth Century
  Society
Victoria and Albert
  Museum
Wadham College, Oxford

**At English Heritage and
Oxford City Council**
Katharine Davies
Katharine Owen
Nicholas Worlledge

WilkinsonEyre
Julia Barker
Rossanna Barreto
Ben Bisek
Sarah Broadstock
Gary Chapman
Ruth Cuenca
Ed Daines
Eleanor Dodman
Julia Glynn-Smith
Ben Hartwell
Christian Hoeller
Leszek Marszalek
Oliver Moore
Andrea Seegers
Rebecca Spencer
Geoff Turner
Andrew Walsh

Contractors
Stewart Basham
Stewart Brooker
Tim Court
Joe Craven
Jim Gillespie
Shane Govern
Steven Harris
Steve Henley
Lee Hutchinson
Rob Jackson
Andrea Joseph
Ryan King
Thomas Masterson
Ivan Metcalfe
Johan Muller
John O'Connor
Terry Spraggett
Keith Thompson
Nick Topham
Keith Vance

**Collaborators and
consultants**
Bernard Antieul
Patrick Antrobus
Tom Ashley
Graham Barber
Anthony Bevis
Janette Blackburn
Graham Burd
Les Chapman
Mihalis Chatzis
Stuart Chown
John Cracknell
Alan Day
David Dehaas
Colin Duke
Patrick England
Gary Fells
Bob Grimwood
Tim Hiscutt
Jonathan Howard
Sandy Howe
Mark Johnson
Darren Kaley
Stuart Kiddle
Richard Lamb
Vivien Lovell
Amanda Morrison
Michael Morrison
Chris Pattison
Brad Rockell
Chris Rolf
Paul Rushbrooke
Shomil Shah
Stephen Stringer
Joe Thornton
Chris Turner
Mark Tutton
Ian Watts
Alexandra Wood
David Young

**And for their assistance
in making this book**
Bodleian Publishing
Claire Cock-Starkey
Samuel Fanous
Emma Keyte
Rachel Malig
Hamish Muir
Andrea Rocco Matta
Deborah Susman
Su Wheeler

The Bodleian Libraries express
their sincere gratitude to both the
many generous donors who have
contributed the funds to enable
the project to be completed. The
project would not have been
possible without the skill,
creativity and commitment of the
many Bodleian staff who worked
on the project over many years.
Richard Ovenden

I would like to thank the
consultant team involved in the
design of this project and also
those who have contributed to the
production of this book. Particular
thanks are due to Geoff Turner
who has steered the architectural
team with the utmost dedication
throughout the life of the project.
I also owe special thanks to
several other key members of the
WilkinsonEyre team: Andrew
Walsh, Leszek Marszalek, Julia
Glynn-Smith and Julia Barker.
Jim Eyre

Image credits

Architectural Press Archive/ RIBA Library Photographs Collection
45 (top right), 51 (top right, bottom left)

Barber Osgerby
193 (sketches), 194, 195

Ben Bisek
19, 25, 27, 29, 34–5, 86 (bottom right), 127 (top right), 133, 138, 142, 149, 161, 177, 178 (right), 179 (bottom), 181 (bottom), 182 (left), 183, 185, 186, 187, 188, 189, 191 (left), 198–9, 201 (top), 202, 205, 207, 210, 211

Bodleian Libraries, University of Oxford
41, 45 (top left), 46, 47, 53, 54, 57, 65, 83 (bottom), 88 (top and centre), 89, 112, 113 (bottom), 140 (left), 146 (left), 148 (top), 150 (left), 178 (left)

James Brittain
14–15, 17, 21, 22, 23, 36–7, 84 (bottom right), 86 (bottom centre), 93, 125, 127 (top left, bottom), 130, 131, 134–5, 139, 144, 145, 154, 155, 160 (right), 182 (right), 191 (right), 196–7, 201 (bottom), 203 (top), 209

John Cairns
24, 26, 203 (bottom), 212, 213

James O. Davies
(for the National Monuments Record)
10–11, 38–9, 78–9, 214–15

Janet Hall/RIBA Library Photographs Collection
51 (bottom right)

hurleypalmerflatt
121

Philippa Lewis/Edifice/Corbis
92 (left)

Mace
170, 171

Will Pryce
28, 30–31, 32–3, 43, 45 (bottom), 76, 77, 92 (right), 141, 152, 153, 158–9, 160 (left), 162–3

RIBA Library
55

RIBA Library Drawings Collection
49, 56, 59, 61 (top)

RIBA Library Photographs Collection
51 (top left), 61 (bottom), 63, 81 (right, top left)

Greg Smolonski
75, 167, 173

Peter Williams
(for the National Monuments Record)
66–7, 164–5, 174–5

Image on page 86 (bottom left) courtesy of the Trustees of Sir John Soane's Museum

All other images and drawings are copyright of WilkinsonEyre

Our thanks to Fiona Orsini, curator of the RIBA Library Drawings Collection, and her team for their help in sourcing original drawings of the building

Images from the National Monuments Record

In 2009, before the decant of the library began, photographers James O. Davies and Peter Williams visited the library to record it in its existing condition for the National Monuments Record.

The NMR was established in 1940 as the National Buildings Record (NBR). With the threat of war, many works of art were moved out of the cities but buildings could not be protected in the same way. The NBR set out to create a photographic record of buildings with historic or heritage value that were at risk of bomb damage. The scope and significance of the NBR continued to grow after the war, with the collections extended to include industrial and commercial buildings, and the name changed to NMR in 1963 to reflect the fact that archaeological records would now also be included.

The NMR was one of the organizations that merged with English Heritage in 1999, which in turn became Historic England in 2015. The collection has now been renamed the Historic England Archive.

The photographs taken show the chaotic beauty and rich patina of the library before its refurbishment, particularly in the bookstack itself, and demonstrate how staff had adapted to the changing demands of readers – and the archival needs of the objects within the collections. A selection of the photographs is included in this book to introduce each section.

A word on the type

Imprint

It seemed appropriate to choose a typeface for this book that would allow Scott's architecture – and the more recent interventions – to speak for themselves. Although an obvious option would be to use Gill Sans, the archetype of the 1930s, and contemporary to Scott's design, we looked elsewhere for a sans serif that would remain in the background and let the content shine.

Unica, commissioned by the Haas Type Foundry and designed by Team '77, was an attempt to create the ultimate sans serif – a hybrid of a family of fonts descended from Akzidenz Grotesk and including Helvetica and Univers. Released to great acclaim in 1980, Unica sadly disappeared from view soon after and was lost to the current digital environment.

Monotype has now revived the typeface, which in the intervening time has gained almost mythical status in the type community, and this book is one of the first to use Neue Haas Unica throughout.

Our choice of Unica for the book is somehow a little like the Weston Library itself: a subtle intervention with quiet character, clean, understated and elegant.

First published in 2016 by the Bodleian Library in association with WilkinsonEyre and Mace Broad Street, Oxford OX1 3BG www.bodleianshop.co.uk

Text © the contributors
Images © as attributed
This edition © Bodleian Library, University of Oxford, 2016

ISBN 978 1 85124 374 7

Editor and Project Manager: Emma Keyte

In-house Managing Editor: Deborah Susman

Designer: Hamish Muir

Production Manager: Nicola Denny for the Bodleian Library

All rights reserved

No part of this book may be reproduced, stored in a retrieval system, or transmitted in any form or by any means, electronic, mechanical, photocopying, recording, or otherwise, without the written permission of the Bodleian Library, except for the purpose of research or private study, or criticism or review.

Printed and bound in China by C&C Offset Printing Co. Ltd on 157gsm Chinese Hua Xia Sun (Golden Sun) matt art.

British Library Catalogue in Publishing Data
A CIP record of this publication is available from the British Library